Youth Deviance
in Japan

JAPANESE SOCIETY SERIES

General Editor: Yoshio Sugimoto

Youth Deviance in Japan

Class Reproduction of Non-Conformity

Robert Stuart Yoder

Trans Pacific Press

Melbourne

This English edition first published in 2004 by
Trans Pacific Press, PO Box 120, Rosanna, Melbourne, Victoria 3084, Australia
Telephone: +61 3 9459 3021 Fax: +61 3 9457 5923
Email: info@transpacificpress.com
Web: http://www.transpacificpress.com

Copyright © Trans Pacific Press 2004

Designed and set by digital environs Melbourne.
enquiries@digitalenvirons.com

Printed by BPA Digital, Burwood, Victoria, Australia

Distributors

Australia
Bushbooks
PO Box 1958, Gosford, NSW 2250
Telephone: (02) 4323-3274
Fax: (02) 4323-3223
Email: bushbook@ozemail.com.au

USA and Canada
International Specialized Book
Services (ISBS)
920 NE 58th Avenue, Suite 300
Portland, Oregon 97213-3786
USA
Telephone: (800) 944-6190
Fax: (503) 280-8832
Email: orders@isbs.com
Web: http://www.isbs.com

Japan
Kyoto University Press
Kyodai Kaikan
15-9 Yoshida Kawara-cho
Sakyo-ku, Kyoto 606-8305
Telephone: (075) 761-6182
Fax: (075) 761-6190
Email: sales@kyoto-up.gr.jp
Web: http://www.kyoto-up.gr.jp

UK and Europe
Asian Studies Book Services
Franseweg 55B, 3921 DE Elst,
Utrecht, The Netherlands
Telephone: +31 318 470 030
Fax: +31 318 470 073
Email: info@asianstudiesbooks.com
Web: http://www.asianstudiesbooks.com

ISBN 1–8768–4317–9 (Hardback)
ISBN 1–8768–4311–X (Paperback)

National Library of Australia Cataloging in Publication Data

Yoder, Robert Stuart.

Youth deviance in Japan : class reproduction of
non-conformity.

Bibliography.
Includes index.

ISBN 1 876843 17 9.
ISBN 1 876843 11 X (pbk).

1. Conflict of generations – Japan. 2. Status offenders –
Japan. 3. Juvenile delinquents – Japan. 4. Social
conflict – Japan. 5. Japan – Social conditions – 1945– .
I. Title. (Series: Japanese society series).

305.2350952

To my children Rummy, Hiro and Ai
and mentors Gene and Patricia

Contents

Tables

Preface

When I began this study twenty years ago, I had little idea of what to expect. At that time there was little information available about Japanese youth deviance and even less about class conflict in Japan. On the contrary, it was the heyday of the harmony model as a way of explaining Japanese society and my fieldwork on class ecology and youth deviance was far from being in vogue.

It was in the field, however, that I first detected signs of what was to come. In interviews, working class youths voiced strong objections to strict adult controls imposed on youth behavior and mannerisms and conveyed a history of turmoil at the local middle school. It became apparent that disadvantaged, working class youth were living outside mainstream Japanese society and that some of them did not care that they had little chance of 'making it' in middle class Japanese society.

Fieldwork in an upper-middle class community revealed a very different scenario. Here youths spoke of lenient adult controls and more conforming social behavior. Combined with other observations in the field, these encounters suggested the emergence of a clear pattern, whereby adult controls over youth varied according to class and that the amount of control influenced the degree of youth rebellion.

After the original research was completed, I continued thinking about these young people and wondered what had happened to them as they had entered young adulthood. This then led to two follow-up studies, which were conducted four and fifteen years respectively after the original fieldwork. Results from these studies were similarly revealing as they showed that class conflict during adolescence is linked to the reproduction of class in the transition to young adulthood.

It was after the second follow-up study, four years ago, that I read Paul Willis's book *Learning to Labor*, about the class reproduction of working class English lads, that I found myself saying, 'Yes, that happens in Japan too.' Despite the obvious cultural differences between England and Japan, the establishment in both these capitalist, democratic societies maintains the 'status quo' through the disregard of the disadvantaged conditions and dignity of the working class. Japanese youth, however, like young people everywhere, are not docile instead they are quite vocal and idealistic. Most of them question, and many rebel against, the smothering constraints of the agents of adult social control and issues of social injustice. This book is their story, a story from which we all could learn.

Acknowledgements

This study began as dissertation research in 1983, mainly under the tutelage of Dr. Gene Kassebaum and Dr. Patricia G. Steinhoff at the University of Hawaii. Not only did Drs. Kassebaum and Steinhoff provide me with the necessary guidance and encouragement to ease the pain of completing a dissertation, but they have also remained my mentors and role models ever since.

In the past few years I have been most fortunate to become acquainted with Dr. Gesine Foljanty-Jost and Dr. Susanne Kreitz-Sandberg, both well respected scholars of Japan in Europe. I am grateful to them for inviting me to participate in a three-day symposium on Japanese youth, held in Halle-Wittenberg Germany in 2001. The contacts and the exchange of ideas and information that took place during the symposium were influential on my writing of this book. I am also very appreciative of the sponsorship provided by Volkswagen in Germany, which enabled me to attend the symposium. I wish also to thank David Slater, Amy Borovoy, Rebecca Fukuzawa and Brian McVeigh for their insightful comments about this research during 'our sessions' together. Brian's reading of and excellent feedback regarding an earlier version of this text led to revisions that, I believe, have made for better reading. Dr Roger Averill, editor for Trans Pacific Press, did an excellent job in editing the manuscript. Professor Yoshio Sugimoto, General Editor for TPP's Japanese Society Series, has given sound advice and direction from the very beginning and his expertise has been invaluable in bringing the manuscript to completion.

Finally, I am deeply indebted and can never thank enough the youths and their mothers in the two communities where I conducted my fieldwork over a sixteen-year period. I had nothing to offer these people except my desire to draw attention to their plight through the writing of this book. I intruded into their private lives, and yet they included me as one of their own. They will always be remembered.

Robert Stuart Yoder
27 April 2004

1 Introduction: Youth Rebellion and Class Conflict in Japan

Youth-adult conflict in Japan

The past two decades in Japan have been characterized by rampant youth-adult conflict. Juvenile delinquent arrest rates for Penal Code offenses dramatically increased in the 1970's and youth arrests for criminal offenses nearly doubled from 1972 to 1983 (White Paper on Police 1984). Rates for status offenses more than doubled during the same period, reaching a postwar record high in 1983, with nearly eight percent of the nation's youth being officially sanctioned for misbehavior (White Papers on Police 1984). From 1990 to 1997, rates of school violence increased three-fold, school absentee rates doubled and school dropout rates spiraled to postwar record highs (Foljanty-Jost 2000a; Montgomery 2002; Seishōnen Hakusho 1999). Clearly, in the past twenty years, adult social controls in Japan have not successfully quelled youth discontent.

This book investigates the reasons why Japanese youths rebel against adult social controls and describes the consequences of this rebellion for youths as they enter young adulthood. Unlike most studies of deviant youth behavior in Japan, this book views the problem through the eyes and experiences of the youths themselves. Interviews with young people, combined with detailed observations of their sometimes criminal behavior and analysis of survey research data will tell a very different story about youth-adult conflict in Japan from that told by the agents of social control (teachers, police, etc.) and the sensationalized version of events portrayed in the mass media.

Adult social controls (including delinquency controls) over youth are more than a means of preventing and punishing their non-conformity. I argue that adult social controls of youth deviance preserve the 'status quo' and actually contribute to the very thing they purport to prevent – youth deviance itself. It will be shown that greater attention and more stringent adult social controls are imposed on working class youths than on their middle and upper class counterparts. These controls are aimed at identifying, tagging, isolating and containing youth deviance rather than reducing youth crime. A longitudinal study (panel design) that traces one group of adolescents into young adulthood demonstrates that the effects of this process flow into adult life.

This study began as research for a Ph.D. dissertation in 1983 (Yoder 1986). My ethnographic fieldwork focused on youth crime amongst lower-middle/working class adolescents (hereafter, to be called 'Minami youth') and upper-middle class youths (to be called 'Hoku youth') in two residential areas of Kanagawa prefecture, southwest of Tokyo. With the initial fieldwork completed in 1985, I conducted a follow-up study of the same youths in fall 1987 and then again, when they were adults, eleven years later, in 1998–99. The original research focused on youth deviance, while the follow-up studies looked at the young people's transition into adulthood, paying particular attention to the impact the subjects' youthful deviance was having on their adult lives.

Youth crime in Japan

Compared to adult crime rates, juvenile delinquency rates in Japan have been quite high. Since the middle 1970's to the most recently released figures in 2001, looking at group population rates per one thousand, there were between three and nearly five times as many youth Penal Code offenders for major crimes as there were adult Penal Code offenders (Keisatsu Hakusho 2002: 138; Shikita and Tsuchiya 1992: 233). From 1980 to 2001, youth offenders accounted for about half of all arrests for Penal Code offenses (Hanzai Hakusho 2002: 180). Rates of pre-delinquency or status offenses are exceptionally high. Consistently from 1980 to 2001, the rate of young people caught and punished for being in violation of these youth-specific criminal acts (e.g., smoking, truancy, gang activity, under-age sex, etc.) has been around five times higher than those arrested for Penal Code offenses (latest figures available in Seishōnen Hakusho 2002: 80–81). This book pays particular attention to status offenses, also referred to as misbehavior or youth crime.

Scholarly literature

Most scholarly work in English on crime in Japan is primarily concerned with adult crime, and often cites Japan's low adult crime rate as a point of contrast for high rates in America (Bayley 1976; Vogel 1980; see Steinhoff 1993 for a critique of such works). While a 'hot topic' in the mass media, juvenile delinquency has received less scholarly attention and the work that does exist is reliant on official statistics or focuses on the characteristics of the juveniles arrested (DeVos and Wagatsuma 1984; Kanazawa and Miller 2000; Shikita and Tsuchiya 1992; Yonekawa 2001). The following short review of existing literature provides an overview of what has come to be accepted as the main causes of and possible solutions for juvenile delinquency in Japan. It also provides a context for my research, suggesting how it variously complements and differs from past studies.

Problems in youth-parent relations have been a popular approach to explaining juvenile delinquency in Japan (DeVos and Wagatsuma 1984; Foljanty-Jost 2000a, 2000b; Hood 2001; Hoshino 1983). DeVos and Wagatsuma (1984) made an extensive review of American and Japanese literature on the family and juvenile delinquency in postwar Japan and applied Gleuck's family scale as a measure of youth-parent discord. Their research in Arakawa ward, a lower class area of metropolitan Tokyo, focused on a small, mixed sample of delinquent (indicated by troubles with the police) and non-delinquent junior high school boys living in intact lower class families. Delinquency was attributed to a weaker family structure, thus delinquent boys were generally found to come from families that lacked cohesion, parental supervision and discipline.

Blame for juvenile delinquency has often been attributed to dysfunctional socialization of excessively protective parents. Foljanty-Jost (2000a) reported that it is common among older academics and educators to equate the problem of delinquency with the tendency for modern parents to overprotect their children and to under-emphasize the need for them to get ahead through education. Most blame is usually apportioned to the mother, who is accused of 'spoiling' the child and thereby creating a self-centered individual with low-level social skills, one likely to pursue a young life of entertainment and leisure. Hood (2001: 149) concurs with this view, saying that 'many juvenile delinquents are found to have been "indulged by their parents" and to be "immature for their age".'

Rapid social change in postwar Japan is said to have created a generation gap within the family, making it difficult for parents to properly socialize their children (Hood 2001). The father's traditional disciplinarian role has weakened and as such young people lack a solid sense of 'right' and 'wrong.' Parents are now thought to be unable 'to communicate with their children and to educate what the [Educational] Ministry calls "sound minds" in children' (Foljanty-Jost 2000b: 5).

Another common explanation for youth deviance in Japan is the pressure for young people to achieve in a very demanding education system (Hood 2001; Hoshino 1983; Schreiber 1997). Delinquency rates are reported to be quite high for youths experiencing trouble at school, those who attain poor academic results and those who fail to complete their high school education.

Osamu (1998) attributes the increased use of drugs among youth and the rise in youth crime during the 1990's as ways of escape from the pressure on young people to perform well in school academics. For seven years Osamu, a senior high school teacher in Kanagawa prefecture, spent whole nights patrolling youth hangouts in Yokohama, encouraging young people to get off drugs. Based on his 'personal patrol' observations and a 1996 survey he did of students at five senior high schools in Kanagawa prefecture, he concludes that drug abuse among young people is a much more widespread and serious problem than adults realize.

Educational reforms designed to combat this supposed increase in youth deviance have received a tremendous amount of national attention from their inception in the late 1970's. In 1980, as spokesperson for the Liberal Democratic Party (LDP), Prime Minister Yasuhiro Nakasone blamed rapid social change in postwar Japan for crippling the ability of schools to provide proper moral training and development of a child's 'whole person.' Sweeping national educational reforms were deemed necessary to reduce high rates of juvenile delinquency and related problems in schools (Fujita 2001; Hood 2001; Kreitz-Sandberg 2000).

Hence, in 1984 Prime Minister Nakasone was the main force behind the establishment of the *Rinji Kyōiku Shingikai* (abbreviated as *kyōshin,* the ad hoc educational council). Moral education was introduced in schools to curtail rising youth deviance. Nation-wide, schools succumbed to the pressure of the *kyōshin*, so that, according to Hood (2001: 83), by 1993 'almost all elementary and lower secondary schools have now drawn up teaching plans for moral education and are using supplementary readers.' In 2002, educational reforms originating from this ad-hoc educational council were implemented nation-wide, a main emphases being on 'moral education,' voluntary student community work and the development of stronger ties between the state, community, family and schools.

Official perspectives on youth deviance have been careful not to contradict the ruling party's (the LDP's) stance on the juvenile delinquency, because, apart from anything else, the National Police Agency is under direct control of the Prime Minister. As such, it is interesting to note that the National Police and Ministry of Justice's annual 'White Paper on Crime's' appraisal of the causes of juvenile delinquency is quite similar to that of the ad hoc educational council.

> After 1975, increases in juvenile delinquencies were largely due to the changing circumstances of an affluent society, increasing diversity of its values among the people, declining attention paid to caring for and educating children on the part of families and local communities, and more opportunities for juveniles to commit crimes (Shikita and Tsuchiya 1992: 234).

Other official perspectives on youth deviance, including delinquency, vary but are consistently conservative in their explanations of causes. The Ministry of Education in 2000 surveyed a large sample of five thousand, five hundred students at twelve different elementary and middle schools in the metropolitan area of Tokyo to look at the relation between stress and aggressive behavior (Taki 2001). They found that the more stress placed upon students (by their family, school and peer group) the more likely they were to exhibit aggressive behavior. Adopting a 'self-inclination' model to explain juvenile delinquency, the official White Papers on Crime (Hanzai Hakusho 1998: 210–222) focused on the motivation of juveniles arrested for committing a crime. From 1975 to 1997, greed was consistently cited as the most common motivating factor for property crimes. The most typical reason given for committing violent crimes (assault related) was anger.

Both scholarly and governmental studies of juvenile delinquency in Japan have rejected social class as a condition worthy of attention.

Even DeVos and Wagatsuma's (1984) above mentioned study of family ties and delinquency among lower class boys in Arakawa ward failed to compare different classes and their youth crime rates. For example, they did not compare crimes committed by lower and middle class youths and totally neglected the issue of female delinquency. In addition to these oversights, the sampling procedure in their study contained a number of flaws. The selection of subjects for the study (young boys) was done by junior high school teachers choosing a small number (fifty) of delinquent (defined as having been in trouble with the police) and non-delinquent lower class students. As the authors themselves admitted, this biased the study because the teachers tended to select 'model students' as representatives of the non-delinquent students (DeVos and Wagatsuma 1984: 61–72). Finally, DeVos and Wagatsuma completely ignored the 'labeling effects' of police contacts and arrests. Remarkably, given these methodological failings and the lack of supporting evidence, the authors concluded that social solidarity and the continuity of strong family ties in lower class communities neutralizes class as a causal factor in youth delinquency in Japan, unlike the situation in the United States.

Kassebaum (1974) recognized years ago the importance of class and other social conflicts to an understanding of delinquency when he stated:

> Delinquency cannot be understood apart from the social conflicts of which it is a part. The most relevant conflicts are those rising along the lines of generation, sex, race, and class. The patterning of delinquency rates is crucially connected to both the legal institutions and rules that mediate efforts at crime and delinquency control, as well as to the informal, or subterranean, or illegal practices of police, courts, and correction agencies in handling youth. [Kassebaum 1974: 1–2]

The long-held myth of Japan being a uniquely homogeneous, middle class society, and therefore lacking class conflict, is, no doubt, largely responsible for the common dismissal of class as irrelevant to studies of Japanese juvenile delinquency. Class is not even mentioned in what Foljanty-Jost (2000a) reports as the three most common approaches adopted by Japanese scholars in the study of youth problem behavior. American researchers, preoccupied with Japan's low adult crime rates, have tended to look at what's 'right' in Japan and 'wrong' in America, perpetuating the 'harmony model' of crime control in Japan.

McVeigh (2002:46–75) goes to some length to argue that Japanese nationalism and ethnocentrism are responsible for the myth of Japan as being a uniquely homogenous society. This has contributed to the tendency, particularly among foreign researchers, to envision Japan as a harmonious whole, dismissing as unimportant social class and other internal differences and conflicts that do not conform to the image of a unified nation. In reference to studies of education in Japan, McVeigh (2002: 27) stated, 'If Japan is a unitary, monolithic, and self-contained unit, then likewise for its educational system. The national state may be useful for certain purposes, and generalizations are sometimes unavoidable, but just the same, it often obscures the actual socioeconomic terrain of societies under study.'

The 'myth,' or as Sato (2001: 30) called it, 'wishful thinking,' of Japan as a unique, middle class society is simply not borne out by the hard data (see Sugimoto 2003: 35–57). Sato (2001: 27) demonstrated that from 1965 onward the number of blue-collar and upper-tier white-collar father-son successions has been roughly the same in Japan as in Britain. The pure mobility rate (removing structural mobility or mobility that occurs because of structural changes of work in society and then calculating inter-generation mobility) in Japan is actually lower than that in both Britain and the U.S. (Sugimoto 2003: 35–36). Among developed nations, Japan ranks somewhere in the middle of income inequality and is near the bottom in both a progressive tax system and the percentage of Gross Domestic Product spent on social security programs (Verba et.al. 1987: 9–12).

The gap between the rich and poor in Japan has widened over the past few decades. Since the 1970s the GINI index (a measure of inequality in income distribution) has increased in value, indicating greater income disparity in the population (Sugimoto 2003: 49). In 1995 the social class structure (as indicated by education, income and occupational prestige) was more consolidated at the top and bottom than it was in 1975 and 1985. This means, for example, that it has become more difficult for persons with a high school education or less to get a good job and higher income than before (Sugimoto 2003: 49–50). Furthermore, the rate of progressive tax has decreased and the value of assets (land, financial holdings, etc.) has increased, thereby widening the capital gain gap between those with and without assets, all of which has made the wealthy wealthier and the poor poorer (Sugimoto 2003: 49–50).

It is against this economic backdrop that some studies have begun to detect a link between class and juvenile delinquency in Japan. In 1983 Rohlen discovered a strong correlation between a family's socioeconomic situation and the rank of the high school (from low to high) that students are able to enter. Wealthier children got into the best high schools, while lower class students gained entry into schools in the bottom tier of the high school rankings. High school sub-cultures were formed by way of this ranking system, resulting in students being labeled according to their school's position in the hierarchy. Rohlen explained that '[t]he [high] school each student enters implies a judgement, and its subculture is a portent of the social world to which he is destined. The label received is nearly indelible' (1983: 134).

Rohlen (1983) reported that delinquency was a problem at the two low ranked high schools in his study but not at the other three higher ranked high schools. Similarly, in the larger school district of Kobe, juvenile delinquent arrests and police warnings (most likely also included citations since a record was kept) was related to high school rank. Rohlen stated:

> High school students arrested or given police warnings (for such delinquent behavior as riding motorcycles, for hanging about in unsavory places, and for behavior leading to criminal acts) come largely from vocational schools or low-ranked private schools. Apparently, about three-quarters of the delinquency in Kobe among seventeen-to nineteen year-olds involves students attending schools in the bottom one-third of the school ranking (1983: 298–99).

Agricultural high schools in Ibaraki prefecture, a major farming area in Japan, occupy the very lowest rank among high schools. These schools are the easiest to get into and therefore attract students who, for academic or behavioral reasons, are unable to get into other high schools. Although not mentioned in Okano and Tsuchiya's (1999) study, it is also very likely that such students come from lower class backgrounds (see Chapter 3). Other students look down on such schools. Okano and Tsuchiya (1999: 103) noted that, 'Students have derogatory attitudes toward agricultural high schools, labeling them "potato schools" or "fertilizer schools"; and some are ashamed of the "agricultural" part of the school name.' Students who attended these schools were often apathetic, generally did poor schoolwork and had high dropout and delinquency rates.

Okano and Tsuchiya (1999: 103–107) detailed the deviant behavior of a counter culture group at an agricultural high school in Ibaraki prefecture in which youth crime was an everyday part of school life.

> "Having a good time" includes vandalism. Students damage desks and chairs and draw graffiti on school property. Classroom curtains are dirty since the boys use the curtains as towels after going to the toilets, forcing the school to buy new curtains every year. They eat lunch (which they bring from home) in the class during the morning break. By the afternoon, the classrooms are full of rubbish which soon accumulates near the "weaker" boys giving teachers a clue about the power dynamics of the class (1999: 104).

Yonekawa's (2001) research questioned the official perspective that class is not a significant factor in juvenile arrests and the punishment of juvenile delinquents. Utilizing data not publicized by the police, he discovered a clear 'class bias' in juvenile arrests and the incarceration of juvenile offenders. In 1998 the ratio of young people from families on welfare relief being arrested was five times greater than that for youths who came from families not on welfare. And, while only three percent of Japanese youth live in a single-parent household, youth from single-parent families represented nearly twenty-three percent of juvenile arrests in 1998. Furthermore, youths sent to detention homes invariably come from families in the lowest social-economic class. The percent of young people in detention homes who came from a single-parent family on welfare relief was twice as high as that among youths arrested (Yonekawa 2001: 3). In overview, this data attested that youths arrested for juvenile crimes are generally from a low social class background and those sent to detention homes typically come from the very bottom of the class structure.

Official statistics of juvenile delinquency loosely define class based on family income, thereby obscuring the relationship between family social class and juvenile arrests (Shikita and Tsuchiya 1992: 249–252). In contrast, when in 1992 Yonekawa (2001) conducted a survey of arrested juveniles in the Kanto area and Shizuoka, Niigata and Nagano prefectures, using their fathers' education and occupation as a measure of social class, he found that those arrested were predominantly from a low social-class family background. Compared with the fathers of a sample of youths not arrested, the fathers of those who had been arrested had, in general, a lower level of education and were more likely to have a blue-collar rather than a white-collar occupation. Eighty-six percent of the father's of arrested youths had a high school education or below, while, in keeping with the national average, forty-two percent of the fathers of youths not arrested were college graduates.

Rohlen (1983) and Yonekawa's (2001) studies both challenge the common assumption that class is unrelated to crime in Japan by demonstrating that in fact, like in other modern industrialized societies, class is a major factor in youth crime in Japan. Like Willis's (1977) ethnographic study of class culture and the misbehavior of English lads, this book presents class culture as an essential part of Japanese youth crime. It will be shown that class ecology or the conditions of class in each area including family social class and class conflict leads to the onset and escalation of youth crime.

Conducting field research

The choice of Minami and Hoku as observation sites was based on the class ecological conditions of youth crime. The study was initially designed to investigate locality influences on youth crime, to ascertain whether or not class ecological conditions were more decisive in accounting for youth crime than influences not directly tied to the location in which the crimes occurred, such as youth-parental attachment. Minami was chosen because it had all the features of a place where young people get into trouble, while Hoku was selected as a point of contrast, for its absence of such features. Selecting and establishing the research in these two communities took considerable time and involved a number of important decisions.

The communities had to be within reasonable traveling distance of my home, so I decided to select two cities with contrasting youth crime rates within the prefecture (Kanagawa) in which I lived. Shonan (the fictitious name I have given to the city in which Minami is located) had a high rate of juvenile misbehavior in 1983, with police actions against youths in the area (and approximately eighty-five percent local residents) being about twice that of the national average. In contrast, misbehavior rates in Kaigan (the name given to the city in which Hoku is located) were not only more than two times lower but unlike Shonan most youths cited for misbehavior acts in Kaigan lived outside of the city (Yoder 1986: 86–91). A conservative estimate would place at least three times more Shonan than Kaigan youths officially apprehended and sanctioned for misbehavior offenses in 1983.

Finding Minami involved a lot of footwork. Having spent many days walking around the city in search of a working class community with an active crime prevention association, I knew I had found what I was looking for as soon as I entered Minami. The community had wall-to-wall housing, with many run-down homes and apartments, its roads were unpaved and there were a number of small shops with back-room apartments in which the merchants resided. A main highway ran parallel to Minami, adding to the noise and pollution. Surrounding the community were factories and large industrial sites. Minami was located near a large entertainment district, through which young people had to pass to get to the train station. Finally, there were numerous delinquency prevention signs posted throughout the community and Minami had a very large and active crime prevention association. All of this suggested a working class community concerned about youth crime and its prevention. Rent in the area was cheap and shortly after discovering Minami I leased a small apartment in the community.

Hoku was the opposite of Minami. There the community was middle verging on upper class. There was no crime prevention association there was thought to be no need. Hoku was located in a scenic mountain range surrounded by historic shrines and temples. The maintenance of the community's roads and parks, etc., was first rate. Most people in the area owned quite large homes. The community was spread out over a much larger area than Minami and therefore had a much lower population density. There was no commercial activity in the community and the nearest entertainment district was quite a distance away.

Despite obvious differences (e.g., working versus upper-middle class, active and inactive crime prevention, etc.) Minami and Hoku are in many ways similar. Both communities have a population of around one thousand inhabitants, they are both located in Kanagawa prefecture about thirty minutes apart by train and both border the Pacific Ocean. The cities in which the two communities are located also have similar sized populations of around two hundred thousand people. Thus, Minami and Hoku are similar in community and city population size, geographical conditions and prefecture politics, policies and laws.

Adult controls as a cause of youth deviance

Official controls over youth have traditionally been seen as the solution to deviant youth behavior rather than as part of the problem. Studies in the literature reviewed above either fail to mention the problems of official controls or perpetuate the view that increased social controls represent an answer to the problem of juvenile delinquency.

Delinquency controls are central to the problem of delinquency in any country. Kassebaum (1974: 2)) recognized this in America when he wrote, 'Delinquency control programs typically embody contradictory mandates that inhibit the accomplishment of any particular objective. Current delinquency control programs are ineffective in reducing delinquency rates and are escalating the scope, scale, and cost of intergenerational conflict.'

If anything, the conflict caused by delinquency controls may even be greater in Japan than in the United States, simply because there are more of them. Mizushima made this point as long ago as the early 1970s.

> In assessing the comparability of material from Japan with that from the United States, we have the impression that official actions in respect to delicts [derelicts] or potential delicts [derelicts] by minors is in some respects more careful and more stringent in Japan than it is in the United States (1973: 331).

Steinhoff's (1984) excellent work on the student movement in Japan is one of the few studies that recognized adult controls as contributing to young people's discontent. The social protests and the growing student movement of the late 1960s were viewed by the government as a threat to its power and legitimacy. The government responded accordingly by increasing social controls in order to discredit the movement and quell the rebelliousness of student participants. A twenty-nine thousand-strong elite police force centered its attention on intelligence and control over the movement, dormant laws became enforced and Japanese corporate employers cooperated with the police by agreeing not to employ ex-student activists (Steinhoff 1984: 175–76, 186–193). These controls, however, had unintended results. Steinhoff (1984: 175) states that, '[T]he result was that the authorities succeeded in shrinking and containing the student movement, but at the same time they helped radicalize a segment of the movement into guerilla and terrorist activity that perpetuated the conflict on new terms.'

Central to the thesis of this book is a recognition that adult social controls of youth deviance contribute to the very problem they attempt to resolve. For example, there is a direct correlation between the amount of police attention paid to juvenile delinquency and the number of juvenile arrests. Ironically, during the days of student protest, the increased police attention given to the student movement resulted in the police having a decreased capacity to enforce juvenile laws. Yokoyama (1989:46) attributes a decrease in juvenile penal code offenders from 12.0 (per thousand) in 1964 to 8.9 (per thousand) in 1969 to the police having to 'cope with a number of leftist movements.' Conversely, increases in youth crime rates from the late 1970's to the middle 1980's coincided with an increase in police numbers, the establishment of police-directed delinquency prevention groups and extensive police-coordinated, community delinquency prevention activities (Yoder 1986; Yokoyama 1989, 1997).

As mentioned earlier, the official perspective on youth crime has interpreted increased juvenile arrest rates as an indication that 'something has gone wrong' with youth and hence the need for social reform. Based on this false premise, and aided by a compliant mass media, the government has gained popular support for a further crackdown on youth. This typically takes the form of new laws that give the government more control over youth behavior. For example, in 1985 the Business Affecting Public Morals law (in Japanese *shin fuzoku eigyō hō*) was passed, thereby increasing police authority to restrict youth behavior in public places.

Over the years, the Japanese government has campaigned against a certain type of youth deviance (e.g., student protest, juvenile crime, bullying, school disorder, etc.) and, having attained public support, then increased social control measures to deal with the 'new threat.' These campaigns, though, are part of the problem. As they change the definitions of youth deviance, they necessarily alter (usually increase) the number of cases and outcomes of such deviance (see Montgomery 2002 and Yoneyama 1999). And, in the process, new reforms are created that often have little to do with the problem they are trying to eradicate. Regarding recent sweeping national educational reforms, Fujita states:

> Unfortunately, however, current policy arguments and reform measures in elementary and secondary education seem to be irrational and deceptive. Proponents of the current reform movement always bring up school disorder and maladjustment problems as well as juvenile crimes and justify the reform measures by saying that they are coping with these problems. But, there is no rational reason or any evidence to show that these problems will be solved by the above-mentioned reform measures. These measures have nothing to do with school disorder problems but much to do with the structure of educational opportunity (2001:9).

Fujita (2001) points to the lack of consideration given to the issue of how official social control measures actually solve youth problems. Official controls have not been held accountable for their efficacy in dealing with the social ills of youth they purport to remedy. The predominant harmony model of social controls in Japan typified by Bayley's (1976) early work on Japanese crime controls and more recently by Hood's (2001) writing on educational reform and youth problem behavior affirms the official perspective and disregards the discriminate way such controls are applied and the conflict inherent to them. While this will be more thoroughly discussed in later chapters, I wish here to briefly highlight the inefficiency of delinquency controls and their class bias as revealed through my research.

The much higher official youth crime rate in Shonan compared with that in Kaigan is indicative of that police surveillance and activity in working class areas is much greater than in middle and upper class districts. Similarly, the presence of a volunteer, adult delinquency prevention program in Minami and the absence of one in Hoku suggests that this too carries a class bias. There was no evidence that the greater amount of delinquency prevention activities in Minami prevented delinquency. On the contrary, such activities increased youth hostility towards adult authority.

Minami youth experienced more police contact and expressed greater discontent towards the police and community delinquency prevention than did Hoku youth (Yoder 1986: 248–253, see also Chapter 2). Most Minami youth thought the police did not understand youth problems. As one Minami girl said:

They are here to protect us, but they don't do it for our safety, they do it because they have to. So when it comes to juvenile delinquency, they simply threaten youth by arresting them, there are few policemen who are willing to talk and listen to youth. I don't like policemen, and I don't trust them. I've never seen a nice policeman in Shonan city, though I don't know about other places (Yoder 1986: 253).

Minami young people were generally not supportive of community delinquency prevention activities, while many Hoku youths were pleased that their community did not have a crime-prevention association some saying there was no need of one. The negative feelings of Minami youths and the conflict that stems from delinquency prevention can be best summed up by an interview I conducted with a sixteen-year old Minami girl.

Interviewer: Are you aware of the delinquency prevention activities in your neighborhood?

Girl: Well I forget [them] even if I hear [about them]. I'm not interested [in them].

Interviewer: Why not? Is it because they have nothing to do with your life?

Girl: It's not that they have nothing to do with my life, but it just seems adults are doing just as they want.

Interviewer: Have you seen any of them?

Girl: I can sometimes tell if a person is from the [crime prevention] association or not.

Interviewer: You often see the posters [crime prevention signs in the neighborhood], don't you? What do you think? Do you think they [the posters] are for your protection?

Girl: I don't know what they are doing it for, but from our [Minami youth] point of view it is just…those volunteers might be doing it for prevention, but it won't work. Kids will just repeat the misbehavior again.

Interviewer: These people sometimes patrol for [crime] prevention. They are like [detective] Columbo [quite popular in Japan at the time]. Do you think such an association can prevent misbehavior?

Girl: I don't think so. The term misbehavior implies discrimination. Their activities [raising her voice in anger] won't do any good at all.

Interviewer: What kind of discrimination?

> Girl: For example, my mother would ask me, "Is that youth a
> delinquent?" I didn't like it, but I would keep quiet. But it
> finally really got on my nerves, so I told her that was
> discrimination. She doesn't say it anymore. They [adults
> involved in delinquency prevention] actually have biased
> views. (Yoder 1986: 121–122)

To get an idea of what happens on delinquency prevention patrols,
I went on a few patrols in and around Minami. Patrols on the
lookout for youth crime in Minami are organized and carried out
by the Minami Crime Prevention Unit. Usually comprising a group
of middle-aged and older men, sometimes accompanied by a
policeman, they patrol the streets, parks and other places (e.g.,
behind shops, etc.) looking for young people committing crimes
such as smoking, drinking or inhaling paint thinner.

On one such patrol, members of the Minami Crime Prevention
Unit, wearing armbands and carrying flashlights, walked the streets,
scoured a nearby park and checked behind the local shops, but all
to no avail. Not one young person was caught 'doing something
wrong.' From talking with patrol members and later interviewing
Minami youths, I gained the impression that the purpose of the
patrols was to give these men something to do. Certainly the patrols
had no effect on the prevention of delinquency.

Pre-delinquency and labeling

Pre-delinquency is a recent adult invention, a social control measure
designed to compel young people to abide by the dominant adult
group's definition of appropriate youth behavior. Youth, but not
adults, are subjected to surveillance, judged and liable for punishment
for committing pre-delinquent offences, some of which (e.g.,
drinking and staying out late) are an everyday part of adult social
behavior. Legally powerless, youths, individually or as a group, have
no way of defending themselves against the injustice of adults
imposing on them a set of behavioral norms labeled as 'pre-
delinquent' and encoded in law as 'criminal.' As a group, juveniles
are the only section of Japanese society subjected to prosecution and
punishment by another more powerful social grouping (i.e.,
dominant group adults). In its targeting of young people as violators
of adult standards of youth behavior, pre-delinquency represents a
particularly volatile example of social labeling (Liska 1987).

These laws lead to youths being stigmatized. For example, if the police make an official report regarding a youth that has been caught misbehaving they are obliged to notify her or his parents. If the young person is employed, their employer will be notified, or if they are studying then their school might be informed of their misconduct (this is more likely if they are attending a middle school, as high schools are generally uncooperative with the police and are therefore usually not informed) (Ames 1981; Clifford 1976). Once caught misbehaving, a young person is more likely to be cited again and pre-delinquent citations correlate positively with later arrests for delinquent acts under the Penal Code (Kiyonaga 1982). The more chronic and/or serious cases of pre-delinquency are prosecuted through the family court and approximately ten percent of youth in detention homes were sent there for pre-delinquent acts (Shikita and Tsuchiya 1992).

Thus the social control establishment facilitates the onset and escalation of deviant youth behavior (including pre-delinquent acts) and provides the impetus for youths to adopt a deviant identity. This, in turn, has consequences for young people's transition into early adulthood, a theme discussed in detail in Chapter 6. The process of participating in deviant behavior, of thinking of oneself as a 'deviant' youth and of exiting adolescence interconnects with adult attempts to socially control youth. Youths that fail to measure up to adult standards of youth behavior and this is largely class-based often rebel and are left with limited opportunities in the adult world.

Measuring youth crime

With the exception of Osamu (1998), the literature reviewed used official actions taken against youth offenders as a starting point for their discussions of juvenile delinquency. Some, such as Hood (2001:149–153), equated the rise of juvenile delinquent arrests with problems at home and in the schools, while others, like DeVos and Wagatsuma (1984), skewed their sample of 'delinquent youth' by defining them as those known to have been in trouble with the police. Too often researchers have made the mistake of equating juvenile delinquent behavior with police arrests of youths for violations of juvenile criminal laws.

Police actions (i.e., arrests and citations) against juvenile offenders are not indicators of criminal youth behavior, instead they reflect police behavior; where the police are (and where they are not), who they apprehend, what crime or crimes they decide were committed and how they treat youths caught violating juvenile law. Rates of juvenile delinquency are 'political,' with the police receiving directives from the Prime Minister's office, via the National Police Agency. The number of police, attention given to certain crimes in certain areas, changes in laws and the extent of public cooperation all interact to produce a given rate of juvenile crime in a given calendar year. Most youths that commit crimes, especially status offenses, are never caught. Without actually knowing how much crime is being committed and who is engaging in it within a given population of youths one cannot legitimately proffer reasons for their criminal behavior.

My data regarding youth crime in Minami and Hoku is based on self-reported acts of misbehavior and personal observation. Knowing exactly the kinds and number of criminal acts committed by youths in these areas, the age when a given youth first engaged in such acts, whether or not they have been officially apprehended for such crimes, and the contexts of youth crime, allows for an informed discussion of the reasons for differences in delinquent youth behavior. Observations of youth crime took place in both districts (see Chapter 2) and additional information about youth crime in both areas was obtained through interviews and follow-up studies that tracked the same youths into their early adulthood.

Original and follow-up studies

From January to late spring of 1984, I interviewed most (41 of 72) young people living in Minami (see Appendix 1 on methodology). Those not wishing to be interviewed were asked to fill out a questionnaire, a request to which most complied. In total, eighty-two percent (59 of 72 youths) of Minami's youth were either interviewed or responded to the survey.

From spring through to late 1984 I interviewed sixty percent (fifty-two of eighty-seven) of Hoku's youth. When combined with returned questionnaires, a very high eighty-four percent (73 of 87 youths) response rate was obtained from all the youth then living in Hoku.

Two follow-up studies were conducted in which the young people interviewed in the original study were contacted again. The first follow-up involved mailed questionnaires and was carried out in the fall of 1987, nearly four years after the first interviews took place. The study focused on changes in the lives of the subjects, who by then were either in their late-adolescence or early adulthood. Questions centered on the transitions from middle school to high school, from high school to work or college and from college to the workforce. There were also similar questions to those asked in the original study regarding misbehavior, school life and so on. Nearly fifty percent, or forty-two of ninety-one youths, completed the questionnaire.

From January 1998 to April 1999, a second follow-up study of the same subjects was undertaken. This research was done fourteen to fifteen years after the original interviews were conducted and eleven years after the first follow-up study. Hence, the original Minami and Hoku youths were now young adults, ranging in age from twenty-eight to thirty-three years old.

The second follow-up study was extremely time consuming, since most of the original respondents no longer lived at their family home. Painstaking efforts were made to find them. I also returned to the communities at that time and embarked on another stint of participant observation, through which I noted the changes that had occurred during the intervening sixteen years.

While the second follow-up took a year and a half to complete, the response rate was quite high, with information obtained on more than eighty percent (74 of 91) of all the youths originally interviewed. The response rate was similarly high in both communities, with thirty of thirty-nine (77%) of Minami youth and forty-four of fifty-two (85%) of Hoku youth being accounted for. Most information was gained through mailed questionnaires and face-to-face interviews. In some cases, where the original participant could not be contacted, family members or friends provided follow-up information.

Both follow-up studies were primarily concerned with change, paying particular attention to the impact that their deviant behavior as a youth may have had on their transition into young adulthood. The questions covered topics such as: education, youth and adult crimes, parental relations, peer group activities, occupations, marital status, memories and impressions of adolescence and, in the second follow-up, if the subject was married, how they got along with their spouse.

This longitudinal panel design enabled the research to precisely track exact changes. All the original participants became individual case studies, and I recorded information regarding about half of these from both the first and second follow-up studies. In the absence of a response to the first follow-up study, information in the original study was combined with data gained in the second follow-up.

The follow-up studies allowed for a reliable assessment of social contexts. Due to the age range of the youths in the original study (14 to 20), it was possible to compare the experiences of the older adolescents with those later experienced by the then younger adolescents. The older adolescents were either in their final year of high school or graduated during the original interview period, while the younger adolescents were either middle school or first year high school students. The social contexts, for example, of high schools and their ranking could now be assessed over time. This was done by seeing if younger students went on to experience a similar school life at the same ranked high school or in some cases, the same high school, as the school life experienced by the older students. As will be seen later, the experiences of students were similar over time, thus the social contexts of high schools by school rank could be treated as a consistent facilitator; varying little over time and having similar contextual influences on individual students.

Chapter outline

Chapter 2 investigates the ecological features of youth crime why is it that Minami young people find themselves in situations more conducive to delinquency than young people in Hoku? The strong relationship between high school rank, class ecology and self-reported misbehavior is discussed in Chapter 3. Chapter 4 provides a detailed description of class culture and the influence of class ecology and adult social controls on the non-conforming (including youth crime) behavior of lower working class youths in Minami and a small sub-set of non-conforming Hoku youths. Theoretical discussion, combined with situational descriptions of the conflict between youths and the adult social control establishment, provides some reasons for the non-conformity of these young people. Also, their current adult status is viewed in the light of their non-conformity as youths.

Chapter 5 turns the tables around by describing the importance of class culture, class ecology and adult social controls to the conforming behavior of middle working class Minami and middle and upper class Hoku youths. Their conformity is seen as very much a product of their families' middle and upper class backgrounds, and is shown to be central to the social reproduction of class as these adolescents become young adults.

Chapter 6 synthesizes the arguments and information presented in previous chapters and presents a labeling conflict perspective of youth deviant behavior, identifying and tracing the consequences of such labeling on their experiences of and opportunities in young adulthood. The in-depth case studies of selected youth in Chapter 7 cover a wide range of individual variations in deviant youth behavior and self-identity based on class ecology. They also demonstrate how confrontations with the social control establishment have influenced the kind of adult lives these people live today. Finally, Chapter 8 summarizes the research findings, discusses the need to include 'inequality' in future research on juvenile delinquency in Japan and proposes changes that would reduce youth-adult conflict.

2 Ecological Features of Minami and Hoku

Ecology and youth deviance

This chapter describes ecological conditions as they relate to the deviant behavior of youths in Minami and Hoku. Rates of self-reported misbehavior are compared between the two locations. Regional contrasts regarding class, recreational areas, delinquency controls, parental relations, peer groups and local middle schools are all highlighted. In the process I will demonstrate that the working class ecology in and around Minami increases opportunities for the youth of that locale to engage in status offenses, compared to those presented to youths living in the upper-middle class environs of Hoku and its surrounds.

Ecological studies

Early ecological studies of slums in major America cities discovered that delinquency rates remained high regardless of the constant inward and outward flow of foreign immigrants (Kassebaum 1974: 53–54). Shaw and McKay's well-known research in Chicago in the 1930's identified a positive correlation between deteriorating living conditions, lower incomes and higher delinquency rates and an area's proximity to the city center. That is, the closer the region was to the center of Chicago, the higher its rate of juvenile delinquency (Adams 1980: 90–91; Kassebaum 1974: 54).

Over the years, ecological studies (also known as the 'Chicago perspective') have continued to be a mainstream school of thought in the study of delinquency in America. However, interpretations of the theory and method are now widely varied (Kassebaum 1974: 53–59; Liska 1987: 59–92). Importantly, related to the approach taken in this book, ethnographic ecological studies of youth crime have contributed to an in-depth understanding of the deviant behavior of youths in lower class areas. Where earlier ecological studies relied on grouped data (area arrest rates, census data, etc.), ethnographic studies saw the fieldworker actually become involved in the lives of people living in lower class areas. This provided new insights into the relationship between class ecology and youth deviance, elucidating the sub-cultural relativity of deviance, the discriminate treatment of young offenders based on class and ethnicity, and the social reproduction of class (Chambliss 1975; Suttles 1968; Willis 1977).

Delinquency and ecology in Japan

Studies of Tokyo have generally found very little correlation between class and delinquency rates. This though is because, with the exception of Arakawa ward, class differences do not neatly conform to ward or district boundaries in Tokyo (DeVos and Wagatsuma 1984; Mizushima 1973). There are, however, poor subsections within wards, like those near the city's major transportation centers, which do have high delinquency rates (Mizushima 1973: 59). These areas feature large entertainment districts that are commonly occupied by gangs. For example, *Kabukichō*, in Shinjuku, is well known for its gang activities (Whiting 2000).

While the literature had long suggested that living near an entertainment district was an environmental influence on youth deviance, it had failed to explain in-depth why this might be so. In order to answer this question I spent one year in what Weiten (2001: 48) calls naturalistic observation, observing youth behavior without intervening in the lives of others in the Shonan entertainment district. Since Minami was located near a large entertainment district and Hoku was not, I thought this might have something to do with the contrasting patterns of youth crime and police contact in the two areas. The results of this part of the research will be discussed later, but for now suffice it to say that not only are entertainment districts popular among youths but that by hanging out in them a young person increases the probability of getting caught doing something 'wrong.'

Ethnographic studies of youth deviance in Japan

Ethnographic studies of youth deviance in Japan vary considerably in tone and perspective. Among them though are two studies of *bōsōzoku* (Japanese youth gangs) which both developed a different way of interpreting their gang members deviance. Sato (1991) did extensive fieldwork with *bōsōzoku* in the Kyoto area, particularly drawing on contacts with about seventy gang members. Using attraction and interaction theories (mainly dramaturgy and Thomas's definition of the 'situation'), the author attributed deviant *bōsōzoku* activities to playfulness, to the gang members' enjoyment in being different, their sense of belonging and that they thought of it as a fun way to pass through adolescence. As for class and later, adult criminal involvement, Sato stated:

> The majority of those who participate in gang activities are from middle-class families, and gangs are rarely involved in illicit underworld activities as groups. It seems obvious that most *bosozoku* youths are engaged in gang activities for the pursuit of excitement and thrills rather than from considerations of gain and profit (1991: 2).

Greenfield in his 1994 book, *Speed Tribes*, included a chapter on *bōsōzoku* based on his personal associations with *bōsōzoku* members in the Tokyo area. Written in a narrative style, Greenfield allowed the reader to view lower class youths rebelling against the adult social control establishment from the perspective of the actors themselves. Commenting on the relationships between class, youth gangs and adult Yakuza criminal activity, Greenfield wrote:

> The bosozoku—speed tribes—are Japan's discontented youth. A little under half of them come from broken homes. They revel in noise and spectacle and disturbing the quiet, orderly operation of Japanese society. But they are more than gangs of delinquents. They are also proving grounds for the Yakuza. Bosozoku gang members perm their hair, dress like wise guys, and drive flashy cars and motorcycles without mufflers, hoping to be noticed by the local gumi, or Yakuza family (1994: 22).

Greenfield (1994: 22) noted that *bōsōzoku* were entrenched in and held its power in the lower class confines of Arakawa ward. Along with the large number of gang members coming from broken homes (associated with being lower class in Japan), Greenfield (1994) suggested that most gang members came from a lower-social class family background. The difference of class (one saying *bōsōzoku* are middle class and the other depicting a lower class family background) actually does not mean much since both field studies did not measure (or at least didn't report on it in their book) the social class of the *bōsōzoku* members' parents. Sato (1991:137–138) addressed the issue of class, but only subjectively. He argued that class was not a conscious motivational factor in a young person deciding to engage in *bōsōzoku* activities. Greenfield (1994: 21–23) wrote about turf domination in a lower class area assuming a rather typical association of gangs coming from and dominating lower class communities (see Suttles 1968). Still, no mention was made of their parent's social class and the origin of the statistic regarding the high percentage of *bōsōzoku* members from broken homes is unclear.

Perhaps the actual parental social-class of *bōsōzoku* lies somewhere in-between both studies. Objective measures of class in Japan consistently show a high correlation of father's social class (education and occupation) and the educational achievement and attainment of their children (Cummings 1980; Fujita 1995; Okano and Tsuchiya 1999; Rohlen 1983; Sugimoto 2003; Yoneyama 1999). Yonekawa's (2001) findings (see Chapter 1) are pertinent to *bōsōzoku* because they revealed a strong negative correlation between the social class of a youth's father (based on occupation and education) and delinquent arrests. In other words, the lower the class the higher the arrest rate. Furthermore, Yonekawa (2001) found that youth incarcerated in juvenile detention homes come from the lowest of all social class backgrounds and incarceration rates for *bōsōzoku* are high.

These findings cast doubt on Sato's (1991) claim that the *bōsōzoku* were predominantly middle class (Sato 1991: 134–5, 159–60), since most of the author's *bōsōzoku* informants were academic failures, nearly all had troubles with the law and about thirty percent had been incarcerated in correctional institutions. While some may very well have been from higher-class families, it seems most likely that the majority came from lower social class families (measured by parents' occupational status and education). Nation-wide, the low academic achievement level of *bōsōzoku* and high arrest rate (Sato 1991: 108–9, 196) indicates that *bōsōzoku* are predominantly from lower class families.

Sato (1991: 2, 7) mentioning that *bōsōzoku* kept away from involvement in underworld activities also wrote that most *bōsōzoku* as adults became *ippan shimin* (ordinary citizens). In contrast, Greenfield (1994) described in detail the association of *bōsōzoku* with adult criminals and estimated that nearly half of *bōsōzoku* join the ranks of Yakuza as adults. While this discrepancy may have had something to do with their different populations of *bōsōzoku* (Sato's group was based in Kyoto while Greenfield's *bōsōzoku* came from Tokyo), Yakuza are involved with and do recruit *bōsōzoku*. At least it follows that *bōsōzoku* are more likely to have contact with Yakuza, either during their time as a member of *bōsōzoku* or later when an adult, than a youth not associated with *bōsōzoku*.

Adopting the perspective of the 'harmony model' of crime controls in Japan, DeVos and Wagatsuma's (1984) fieldwork dealt with an array of youth deviant behavior in Arakawa ward, a lower class area of Tokyo. Made popular by Bayley (1976), the 'harmony model' – which presents Japan as a success story in controlling crime – is represented today in work such as Kanazawa and Miller's (2000) social order theory regarding Japan's comparatively low official crime rate. While DeVos and Wagatsuma (1984) devoted a good portion of their book to detailing family problems and their relationship to delinquency, other sections, particularly the conclusion, celebrated the supposed success of Japanese adults in managing, correcting and containing wayward youth behavior in a lower class area. They asserted that adult controls of youth behavior in lower class areas like Arakawa are successful because of harmonious interpersonal relations among Japanese.

> There is little sense of alienation related to authority in Arakawa ward. Authority figures are conceived as part of the community not separate from it. The police in Arakawa are not seen as an occupation force; they have personal relationships with the individuals and families living there. They communicate directly with the teachers and parents. They do not show the impersonality or the interpersonal hostility that occurs in the United States between the police and minority individuals in lower-class neighborhoods (1984: 459).

In method and theoretical outlook, Letendre's (2000) study of adolescent behavior (including deviant behavior) among Japanese middle school students falls somewhere between Sato (1991) and Greenfield's (1994) studies of *bōsōzoku* and DeVos and Wagatsuma's (1984) work on youth deviance. While most information was obtained from school staff (e.g., principals, teachers, school nurses, etc.), the author also observed the daily practices of two Japanese middle schools and compared these with his observations of two American middle schools. The study's ethnographic account of school controls appraised the efficacy of the different schools' abilities to manage student behavior. Letendre (2000: 102–3) highlights the preoccupation of Japanese teachers with regulating and controlling every aspect of their students' lives, from how they wear the school uniform to patrolling places outside of school for evidence of student misbehavior. Japanese teachers held the conventional view that such strict controls helped to prevent the onset of delinquency and that adolescents from a single parent and/or low socioeconomic family were the most likely to exhibit anti-social behavior and delinquency at school (Letendre 2000: 119–120, 135–139).

Obviously, the perspective adopted in an ethnographic study is determined by the involvement of the ethnographer with the people whom are the focus of the study. Hence, Greenfield (1994) and Sato (1991) represented youth rebellion from the viewpoint of the youth themselves, while DeVos and Wagatsuma (1984) presented the adult point of view (mainly police, probation officers, and volunteer adults involved in delinquency prevention) in their depiction of community and official controls of youth deviance. And even though Letendre (2000) astutely observed daily life in Japanese middle schools, most of the data was gained from school officials rather than students. Of course, my fieldwork too has a bias, one towards the youths whose lives I observed. This was a self-conscious methodological decision, made partly in response to the dearth of ethnographic accounts of Japanese youth behavior and partly to address the oversight regarding class as a condition of youth deviance in Japan. Also, it seemed obvious that if we want to know why youth behave the way they do we should seek answers at the source, from youths themselves rather than from adults.

The concept of deviance

Some years ago, Kassebaum, in his landmark work, 'Delinquency and Social Policy' (1974: 69), clearly demonstrated the relativity of deviance, arguing that it is ludicrous to assume there is a society-wide consensus on values and norms. Deviance is not a status but rather part of a process by which '[t]he terms norm, labeling, enforcer, and deviance define deviance as conduct labeled as undesirably departing from a norm that the labeler believes should apply to the deviant, for which enforcement is potentially available' (Kassebaum 1974: 70]. Conflict over definitions of normative youth behavior is inevitable given variations in group values and norms and differences in the amount of power used to enforce what are deemed appropriate standards of conduct.

In this book, deviant youth behavior is treated as being relative to the sub-cultural and class context in which it occurs. It is also seen as a form of youth rebellion against adult authority. Deviant youth behavior is not limited to crimes but also includes behavior that is either subject to non-criminal adult punishment or brings about strong adult disapproval. Such behavior includes violation of school rules, poor academic achievement, hanging-out at game arcades, dating, public displays of affection with members of the opposite sex, or even dress sense and mannerisms.

Class ecology and the two communities

A major weakness of the ethnographic method is its weak ability of control. Doing fieldwork in a lower class community does not enable one to determine with any certainty that it is class and not some other condition that accounts for the youths' deviant behavior, since there is no point of comparison. Thus my decision to conduct similar, comparative fieldwork in Hoku, which differed significantly in its class ecology from Minami. Following the logic of experimental design (Takane 1979), youth in one community (Minami) were exposed to the situations and conditions of the working class while youth in the other community (Hoku) were not. By keeping class a constant I was able to clearly differentiate between factors that were class-related and those that were not. For example, by controlling for class I could ascertain whether or not non-class situations (e.g., youth-parent relations) account for youth deviant behavior over and above class conditions (e.g., parents' socioeconomic status). Finally, the follow-up studies enabled me to track changes over time and thereby find out whether or not the youths' transitions into early adulthood were directly related to class ecology or were a more random outcome of social mobility.

The different sights, smells, sounds and available space in the two communities were integral to peoples' everyday experiences of Minami and Hoku. Though much of it evades direct measurement, the physical environment has an affect on the behavior and lifestyle of people living in a given area. One outstanding ecological difference between the two study sites was the comparative lack of living space in Minami, which had a population density roughly six times greater than that in Hoku.

People were crammed close together in Minami, with few homes offering much space for their inhabitants. Nearly every home, apartment building and shop were in close enough proximity for the inhabitants to know something about the lives of their neighbors. The area was a flat suburban mix of dirt and concrete, with most of the buildings in need of renovation. On two of its four sides, heavy traffic polluted the air, its thundering noise impeding natural conversation. Surrounding Minami were towering *danchi* (large apartment complexes), an enormous hospital, a school for physically disabled children and a smattering of bars, gamble shops and run-down stores. Just a short walk away was a large entertainment district that had to be passed through in order to reach the train station.

In contrast, most houses in Hoku were larger and were well spaced from one another, with front and back lawns, gardens and private parking spaces. Nearly every family in Hoku had at least one car and some residents drove expensive imported cars like BMWs or Mercedes Benz. Hoku was set in very scenic surrounds. Its gardens, trees, hills, historic landmarks, small forest, squirrels and birds, combined with the absence of shops and its meticulous up keep, gave it the appearance of a treasured national park. Just outside of Hoku were numerous shrines and temples, a mountain range, a small commercial shopping area and the local train station. The air was clean and carried the sweet fragrance of nature. It was a quiet place; the most frequently heard noises were the sounds of children playing, neighbors quietly chatting, birds chirping.

The physical and contextual properties of class ecology amenable to measurement relate to the social structure of an area and the background of its residents. Class ecology, as measured in this book, includes family social class, the presence or absence of delinquency prevention organizations, the standard of local middle schools and high schools and the types of recreational areas. The remainder of this chapter discusses these features of class ecology and their relation to youth deviant behavior.

Family background, class and area

Social class can be measured both subjectively and objectively. In Japan there exists a large discrepancy between subjective and objective interpretations of social class. While about ninety percent of Japanese self-identify as middle class, objective measures identify nearly thirty percent of the population as unskilled or semi-skilled workers, that is, lower class (Reischauer 1977: 160). Also, overall, class stratification is roughly the same in Japan as in other modern industrialized capitalist societies (Sugimoto 2003: 35–57). In this study I have chosen to use objective measures of class, mainly because youths are not generally cognizant of their families' social class, but also because it is more the condition of class rather than their perception of it that effects their lives. What follows are the details of the objective measurement of the youths' family social class made in the original study. (A discussion of class based on added information gained in the follow-up studies occurs in Chapters 4 and 5.)

While thirty-four percent (13 of 38) of the fathers of Minami youths had working class jobs (i.e., were operators of small shops or blue-collar workers), none of the Hoku fathers were employed in such work. Conversely, twenty-six percent (15 of 58) of the fathers of Hoku youths were professionals or held company managerial positions, compared with only three percent (1 of 38) of the fathers of Minami youths. Furthermore, while most fathers in both communities were white-collar workers, indicators such as the higher educational levels of Hoku fathers suggested that they had higher status positions and were employed at larger, more prestigious companies than their Minami counterparts.

Another factor indicative of a Minami youth coming from a working class family was if his or her mother was in the workforce, which suggested family financial problems. Seventy-nine percent of the mothers of Minami youths worked, compared to just twenty-five percent of their Hoku equivalents, with nearly five times more Minami mothers working full-time.

The working class status of Minami youth is further indicated by differences in the composition of households there compared with those of their Hoku neighbors. In line with middle class standards, most Hoku youth (65%) lived in a one or two child nuclear family. However, only a little more than a third of Minami youth (35%) came from a one or two child nuclear family. And eighteen percent of Minami youth, compared to only four percent of Hoku youth, came from a single-parent family. Minami youth had more siblings than Hoku youth, with about twice as many having two or more brothers and sisters.

Misbehavior offenses, rates and characteristics

Misbehavior offenses, also called pre-delinquent offenses, status offenses or youth crime, are considered criminal acts under Japan's Penal Code and apply only to youth (Ames 1981: 77; Criminal Justice in Japan; Kiyonaga 1982). In the original interviews and the first follow-up study, respondents were asked to check their past behavior against a list of misbehavior acts (Kiyonaga 1982) and to register when and at what age they first engaged in the various activities and whether or not the police had apprehended them for these offenses. They were also asked whether or not they had been caught misbehaving by a crime prevention association. In the original study, youths also reported on acts of misbehavior committed by their closest friends. Then in the second follow-up study they were asked to name the misbehavior acts they had engaged in as adolescents. During the interviews, they also talked about youth crime in and around the area in which they lived and discussed what they did for fun with their best friends. Hereafter, in this book, their self-reported misbehavior will be referred to as acts of misbehavior, status offenses or youth crime.

Minami youth committed more acts of misbehavior than Hoku youth; averaging three such acts compared to the Hoku youths' two. Minami youth had a higher average of misbehavior acts at each age, from fourteen to nineteen years old. While both boys and girls in Minami engaged more often in acts of misbehavior than their counterparts in Hoku, the greatest difference was between the girls. Minami girls were active in misbehavior reporting 4 or more offenses nearly three times more than Hoku girls did. Thirty-six percent of all Minami girls were actively involved in misbehavior, compared to only fourteen percent of Hoku girls.

Hoku youth were, on average, nearly a year older than Minami youth. Age positively correlated with self-reported acts of misbehavior – as age increased so did the average number of misbehavior offenses. Table 2.1 (taken from Yoder 1986: 97) below lists the age of youths and acts of misbehavior. With the exception of fourteen years of age, when no youths reported misbehaving, at each age level Minami youth average between 1 and 2.6 more acts of misbehavior than Hoku youth. Particularly telling is that the percentage of Minami youth aged sixteen or older actively engaged in acts of misbehavior (4 or more acts) is about twice that of Hoku youth in the same age bracket.

Table 2.1   Rate comparisons of conduct violations between Minami and Hoku youth

Age (years)	Mean number of acts of misbehavior		% reporting 4 + acts		Total number of cases	
	Minami	Hoku	Minami	Hoku	Minami	Hoku
14	0	0	0	0	9	7
15	1.7	0	0	0	3	7
16	3.4	0.5	40	0	10	6
17	4.2	3	44	25	9	8
18	5	4	50	27	4	11
19	5.8	3.2	100	31	4	13
					39	52

Misbehavior occurs in peer groups. When interviewed, youths from Minami and Hoku all reported that their best friends (peer group) engaged in roughly the same amount and kinds of misbehavior as they did. Although frequencies were higher for Minami youth, both youth groups engaged in the same, most common types of misbehavior. Beginning with the act most frequently committed, self-reported misbehaviors by these youths were: cigarette smoking, drinking alcohol without parental permission, curfew violations, truancy, reading pornographic magazines, visiting *pachinko* (gambling) parlors and having sexual relations.

Minami youths began misbehaving at a younger age than their Hoku counterparts. A fair number of Minami youths, but very few from Hoku, committed youth offenses while still at middle school age. Minami youths also reported more aggressive forms of misbehavior. A higher percentage of them reported acts such as: harassing others in public, aggressively arguing with others, being physically aggressive towards another person and associating with a youth gang.

Not only were Minami girls considerably more active in misbehaving than Hoku girls, they were also more 'hip.' Three times (64% compared to 20%) more Minami girls both dated and hung-out at game centers than Hoku girls. Also, Minami girls that either dated or hung-out at game centers did so at a younger age, the average being thirteen and half years old, or nearly two and half years younger than the average age of just below sixteen years old for Hoku girls. This suggests Minami working class girls were more precocious and daring in their behavior than upper-middle class Hoku girls.

Excluding middle school students that did not respond to the first follow-up study, taking all self-reported acts of misbehavior in the original and first follow-up study, Minami youth reported on the average 4.8 acts compared to 3.6 acts of misbehavior for Hoku youth. In all likelihood, the misbehavior rate of Minami youth was even higher than this, because the largest number of non-respondents in both follow-up studies were those Minami youths most actively misbehaving at the time of the original study. Quite a few of these were middle school drop-outs or 1st and 2nd year high school students attending low ranked high schools and it seems reasonable to assume that, like the older adolescent cohort, they later committed an increasing number of acts of misbehavior.

Observing misbehavior

In urban areas in Japan, entertainment districts, often located near train stations, is where the 'action' is. Greenfield's (1994) descriptions of disco life, Kiyonaga's (1983) depictions of youth delinquent groups and Whiting's (2000) detailed history of gang activity are all set against the backdrop of entertainment districts. Entertainment districts are also where police pursue youth crimes, hence the high rates of delinquent arrests in such areas (Ames 1981; DeVos 1973; Yoder 1986).

At the time of the initial study, the Shonan entertainment district was bustling with activity. It boasted numerous *pachinko* (pinball gambling) and *majan* (Chinese style gambling) parlors, game centers, bars, clubs and cabarets. Living near the Shonan entertainment district, many Minami youths hung-out there, but this had nothing to do with them misbehaving more than Hoku youth. Youths from both communities sought fun in entertainment districts, with Hoku youths often traveling to far away up-market districts like Roppongi and Shibuya in Tokyo.

Police and delinquency prevention activities

The police kept a close watch over youth in the Shonan entertainment district. They patrolled places where they suspected young people misbehaved (game centers, fast food outlets, and the streets) and sometimes randomly stopped them as they passed through the district. This resulted in Minami youth having more contact with the police than did Hoku youth.

Since Hoku is an upper-middle class community, one located near historically significant temples and shrines, the police were rarely seen there. The chances of a Hoku youth encountering a policeman on the journey from their home to the train station were extremely remote. The chances were much higher for a Minami youth making a similar journey. Not only were Minami youth more likely to encounter police and community crime prevention patrols near their homes, they also had to pass through the Shonan entertainment district on the way to the nearest train station. The higher rate of police contacts was not something Minami youth liked.

Most Minami youth had at some stage been stopped in the entertainment district or closer to home under suspicion of having done something wrong. Of these, some were written up and cited for misbehavior and a few were arrested. Reasons for police contact with Minami youth included: shoplifting, truancy, smoking, causing a disturbance, breaking the curfew, suspected motorbike theft, illegal riding a bicycle (i.e., two people riding one bicycle) and random checks and questioning as to why they were in a certain area at a particular time. Minami youth did not like being accosted by the police, particularly when they were doing nothing wrong. Consequently, they voiced more negative opinions about the police than Hoku youth.

In the countless times I have frequented entertainment districts, young people have represented the least threat or annoyance to others. Drunk adults have caused the most disturbance, both in the bars and clubs and afterwards, making noise in the streets. Also, con artists often targeted young girls, trying to sell them some scam or other (usually fashion related) or to recruit them for entertainment, often sex-related, work. From my experience it is adults, not youths, who are the real troublemakers in entertainment districts.

The communities

Both the Minami and Hoku communities had a *chōnaikai* (community association) and thereby exercised the normative means of community control in Japan or what Sugimoto (2003: 271–275) refers to as 'friendly authoritarianism in surveillance.' While *chōnaikai* provide important community services, such as clean-up campaigns, helping the elderly (*rōjinkai*), warnings and directives regarding impending typhoons, etc., they also act as quasi-governmental social control units (Ames 1981: 41–43; Sugimoto 2003: 273–275). A sub-group within the *chōnaikai* called *bōhankai* (crime prevention association) acts in liaison with the police and other crime prevention units (such as schools and citizen voluntary groups) in order to control crime within and around its community (Yoder 1986: 12–19). Reflecting differences in their class ecology, Minami had a very active crime prevention organization, while Hoku did not have a crime prevention association at all.

The vigilante tactics employed by Minami's crime prevention association created local distrust of Minami youth. Such tactics were opposed by some adults and almost universally disliked by the region's youth. The Minami Crime Prevention Association did not prevent juvenile delinquency.

The Minami Crime Prevention Association and an affiliate crime prevention organization called 'Youth League' paid particular attention to youth crime in and around the community (Yoder 1986: 86–90). Both associations coordinated their activities with the police and city delinquency prevention groups and organizations. On supermarket windows and telephone poles throughout Minami posters implored citizens to call the police if they saw a child or adolescent doing something wrong, reinforcing the message that juvenile delinquency was rife and had to be stamped out. Public meetings were held at which speakers criticized the loose, deviant and irresponsible ways of youth. Crime prevention association members patrolled the neighborhood hoping to catch kids misbehaving. And yet not one Minami youth was caught misbehaving by one of these patrols. This was probably because, as one local young person said, the youths found places to misbehave that the association did not know about.

Numerous Minami youths commented on their dislike of the preventive delinquency activities. Most Minami youths objected to their neighbors snooping around on the grounds that it was none of their business or that such surveillance only increased tensions between adults and youths. As the following comments of one Minami boy suggests, the negativity of these preventive delinquency activities served only to stigmatize and label young people. 'The neighbors are prejudiced. If they decide that a youth is "bad" then he is thought of only as a person who does bad things. They do not recognize anything else about that youth except that he is a "bad person"' (Yoder 1986: 253).

Hoku youth did not share this dislike for community preventive delinquency tactics simply because they did not have a crime prevention association in their community. Many Hoku youth felt their community did not need a crime prevention association and the absence of one seemed to strengthen trust between them and their neighbors.

Youth-parent relations

The strength of youth-parent relations was assessed via questions asking youths how well they felt they got along with their parent(s). These questions were conceptualized according to social control theory (see Kassebaum 1974 and Liska 1987). Quite popular among Japanese researchers, this theory maintains that a close relationship with parent(s) inhibits a youth from engaging in acts of misbehavior. For control theorists, the question is not why some young people commit crimes, but why others do not. Committing crime can be an exciting, fun and rewarding experience, so what deters young people from doing it? The assumption is that a youth that enjoys close relations with his or her parent(s) is more likely to share their social/cultural values and will avoid criminal activities so as not to disappoint them and thus lose the trust built up between them over the years. A close parent-child bond also keeps the child away from opportunities to engage in unlawful behavior (e.g., joining a youth gang). However, according to the findings of my research, this main tenet of control theory – youth-parent attachment – contributed little to an understanding as to why some youths got into trouble and others did not.

Asked a number of control theory-type questions about their relations with parents, the youths gave responses that failed to support the theory of close parental attachment as a deterrent to youth criminal activity (see Chapters 4, 5 and 7). Discussed in Chapters 4 and 5, working class youths got along as well with their parents as did their higher-class contemporaries, yet their misbehavior rate was twice as high. Whatever the approach, youth-parent relations seemed at best to have a weak and tenuous relationship to youth crime.

Friendships at school and in the community

All Minami youths attended the local middle school. Their best friends either lived in Minami or in a nearby neighborhood. In contrast, nearly half of all Hoku youths attended expensive, private, high status middle schools, thus their circle of friends encompassed a wider area. The other half of Hoku middle school students attended the local middle school and, like their Minami counterparts, their closest friends lived in the community or in an adjacent neighborhood.

After middle school, friendships and peer groups were determined by the high school a student attended, though some youths maintained earlier friendships, some from as far back as kindergarten. Middle school students are channeled according to academic achievements into variously ranked high schools. With the exception of students attending private middle schools, which have interconnecting high schools, this system breaks up middle school friendship networks. Despite this, most Minami students did not develop friendships beyond their home city because nearly half of them were middle school graduates or attended local low ranked high schools and though most that attended higher ranked high schools did so outside the city, a few went to Shonan higher ranked high schools (see Chapter 5). Peer groups are formed at the different high schools that students are sent to and thus peer groups and the group's subsequent strong influence on the behavior of its members are grounded in the high schools not in the community.

Friendships are more important during adolescence than at any other time in our lives. Adolescence is a time of searching for an identity. This often results in acts of rebellion and expressions of idealism as young people are distant from parents and adults in general (Erickson 1978; Weiten 2001: 456–461). My research confirmed that during adolescence a youth's peer group exerts more influence on his or her behavior than does anyone else, including his or her parent(s).

Typically, youths with similar family and class backgrounds and orientations toward academic achievement and conformity became a part of the same peer group. This differed by area and the middle schools the youths attended and had a profound influence on the likelihood of them misbehaving.

The first step toward adolescent conformity or non-conformity was taken at middle school. It was there that lower working class Minami youths became part of a counter-school culture, one in reaction to a 'middle class school value system' that did not fit their class culture (for more details see Chapter 4). In contrast, in Hoku, half of the middle school students became part of an elite peer group formed at private middle schools, where conformity was universal. Middle working class Minami youths were confronted with conflict at the local middle school, but often managed to stay out of trouble by making friends with similar, conformity-minded students. Local middle school students in Hoku did not have to choose between a counter school culture and a more conforming one because rebellious student groups did not exist at their school. Instead there was very little student-school conflict and though students varied slightly in their conformity to school rules and expectations, the peer groups they formed all held middle class values in which conformity to the school was expected and respected.

Local middle school

Middle schools set the pattern for future adolescent misbehavior. The local middle schools attended by Minami and Hoku students could not have been more different. The appearance alone of the Minami local middle school, surrounded by high walls, sections of barbed wire and run-down facilities, gave the impression of a juvenile reformatory rather than a middle school. Staff at the school acted as though they did not want outsiders to know what happened behind those walls. After five requests to talk with teachers and the principal of the school, I was finally granted permission to enter the school. Even then, though, they offered little information and soon asked me to leave. Actually, they politely but firmly threw me out.

By pure chance, I happened to meet the Minami middle school guidance counselor at the bar in a restaurant in Minami. In talking with him and from my interviews with Minami youth (all of whom attended the local middle school) I built up the following picture of the turmoil that took place at the school.

The Minami middle school had a bad reputation for rampant student misbehavior and teacher-student conflict. Students were known to inhale paint thinner and smoke cigarettes in the classroom. Pranks were an everyday reality. For example, students regularly hid other student's shoes (students took off their shoes near the entrance of the school building). First year students feared third year students and dared not disobey them. Teacher-student relations were at best compromised. Students felt that some teachers were simply going through the motions of teaching in order to keep their job. When things got really out of hand, teachers formed a circle around the students to prevent them from leaving the school. The police had been called to the school and the school was reported on in the newspaper for its student violence. The local Minami middle school was said to have the worst reputation of all middle schools in the city.

In stark contrast, the impression gained from staff and students attending the local Hoku middle school was that the school was a warm, trusting and open place in which the students could study. After just one phone call, I was invited up to have a look at the school and a meeting was arranged with the school principal, head teacher and school guidance counselor. Located on the side of a mountain, the newly built school featured many windows and was filled with light and open space. There were no threatening walls enclosing it. Students liked the school and the only problem mentioned was that some students tended to look down on the small minority of students from single-parent families.

The atmosphere of elitism produced by the private middle schools attended by about half of all Hoku youth further underlined the area's privileged social class. Private middle schools are expensive and competition to enter can be fierce particularly at elite upper ranked middle schools. Successful entry into the better private middle schools requires an extremely regimented study program (including *juku* translated as cram or preparatory schools and private tutors) beginning as young as three and four years of age. Many of these schools and their affiliated high schools have direct links with prestigious colleges and the top-ranked middle schools succeed in placing a good percent of their students in the best universities in Japan.

Disadvantaged Minami youth (many of whom are from single parent families and the lowest class background) began misbehavior activity when in middle school. Class disadvantage, combined with them not keen to adhere to a rigid 'middle class' school value system, prompted them to join in with a counter school culture group. Both girls and boys rebelled against school and adult authority by smoking, drinking, skipping school, going to game centers and dating. They did poor schoolwork and either finished their education after middle school or entered low ranked high schools (see Chapter 3); places further marked by student rebellion.

The situation for Hoku middle school students was radically different. Students at private middle schools were conformists and high academic achievers on a path to entering a good, affiliated high school, then college. As such, they reported the lowest rate of misbehavior – almost none. Hoku students at the local middle school were a bit more adventurous and did not do quite so well in their schoolwork. Still, nearly all conformed to school rules and requirements and few reported any acts of misbehavior. Hoku students at both private and public middle schools were more oriented towards and far better prepared for entrance into good high schools than the working class Minami students.

This, then, was a major turning point in the lives of Hoku and Minami youths. In the next chapter I will show how more Hoku middle school students went on to higher ranked high schools than did Minami middle school students and how high school rank strongly related to the likelihood of a youth engaging in acts of misbehavior.

3 Class Ecology, High School Rank and Misbehavior

The harmony model

The effect of class on education in Japan has not received the attention it deserves. Instead, Japan's education system has for many years been praised, particularly by foreign researchers, for its uniform curricula, dedicated teachers, group orientation and high academic achievement in mathematics and science (Christopher 1984; Kanazawa and Miller 2000; Vogel 1980). As mentioned earlier, the harmony model has dominated discussions of post-war Japanese society and education has been seen as central to its success.

The enormous influence of the harmony model on research of both education and deviance in Japan demands that I briefly outline the history of this theory. The harmony model, also called *nihonjinron* (theories of being Japanese), emphasizes the uniqueness of Japanese culture and within that, the social priorities given to conformity, complimentary senior-junior relationships and group orientation. This approach to understanding Japanese society gained popularity in the 1970's characterized by Chie Nakane's well-known book, *Japanese Society* (1970). Nakane insinuated that all Japanese share a common set of cultural norms and values and all have an equal chance of succeeding in life. Regarding education, Nakane stated:

> The way in which a university plays an important role in determining the place of an individual in Japanese society is well illustrated by the normal undergraduate procedure and progress. The university entrance examination is an open and free competition, and universities, particularly those of the highest rank, resist any form of bribery or special favor. The wealth, status and so on of parents are completely disregarded (though this is not always so of second-rate universities). Admission to a university by success in its entrance examination places an individual firmly within a somewhat caste-like system. Among the students of the

University of Tokyo, for example, there are probably sons of farmers, workers, wealthy businessmen and professors, but they stand on a completely equal footing simply because they have gained entry into the University of Tokyo; and ever after they belong to a kind of social clique as 'graduates of the University of Tokyo' (1970:112).

Even the grueling examination system is here described in a harmonious way, as a functional means of social adaptation. In *Japanese Patterns of Behavior* (1976), Lebra portrayed the 'examination system' for adolescents as abetting a smooth transition of a group identity shift from the family to one's peer group (32–33). Similarly, Vogel's popular *Japan as No. 1* (1980) gave high marks to the Japanese educational system for student homogeneity, superior national standards of education and the tenacity of teachers, families and students to work together to achieve academic success. Not to be outdone, later in the 1980s, Christopher made a comment about Japanese education that I believe is still commonly held to be true by many, particularly Western, students of Japan.

[…] some of the most powerful forces for uniformity in education are not matters of government decree but flow naturally out of the culture— specifically, a deeply ingrained reluctance to publicly stigmatize or embarrass anyone. There is, for example, no "tracking" in elementary and secondary schools in Japan; in every classroom, the slow learners are mixed right in with the gifted. And throughout the nine years that Japanese children are legally required to attend school—in other words, in elementary and junior high schools—automatic promotion from grade to grade, regardless of a child's academic performance, is the unchallenged rule (1984: 73–74).

In the new millennium, Kanazawa and Miller (2000) employed their social order theory of solidarity to explain and describe the high degree of conformity in Japan. Typifying the harmony model, they wrote that conformity is a trademark of schools in Japan, that Japanese schools socialize students into a group-like setting, that students participate in the same activities and that teachers treat all students the same (27–29). Believing all students have the same chance, Kanazawa and Miller further postulated that student conformity was a result of the practical importance to perform well academically.

[…] at a fairly young age, Japanese adolescents are made aware of the consequences of not performing well in school. In essence, school work will determine Japanese students' entire future. In other words, there are no alternatives to success other than good academic performance. Thus, behavioral conformity can still be expected based on dependence, but the dependence is no longer purely psychological, a function of socialization; it is now enforced by pragmatism. There is no other route to success other than by following school rules and doing what one is told (2000: 29).

A new approach

While the harmony model paradigm no longer dominates as it once did, Sugimoto (2003: 17) notes that it remains influential in the nation's intellectual life. Added to this, the voluminous English language material promulgating *nihonjinron* continues to mislead non-Japanese students and scholars into believing that they should be looking for 'something unique' in Japanese culture. Citing ample documentation, and with the support of detailed research findings, Sugimoto (2003) refuted the idea of *nihonjinron* by clearly demonstrating that class stratification, regional diversities, subcultures, ethnic minority groups and popular culture in Japan exhibit the same degree of heterogeneity and inequality as in other modern, capitalist societies. The reality of the education system, too, is far removed from the harmony model myth of egalitarianism.

In the English language literature, the subject of the relationship between class and education in Japan received attention by Cummings (1980) and Rohlen (1983) in the early 1980s. More recently, the hierarchical structure of education and the authoritarian nature of school controls, the inequalities and the subsequent problems of student behavior (e.g., school phobia) have come to scholarly attention (Fujita 1995; Okano and Tsuchiya 1999; Saito 2001; Sugimoto 2003; Yoneyama 1999). This trend away from the harmony model of education taking a non-assuming critical approach deserves greater exposure.

Cummings (1980) and Rohlen (1983) both demonstrated that class was an advantage in gaining access to the best secondary schools. This then accounts for the disproportionately high number of middle and upper class students who pass college entrance exams, especially those for the more prestigious universities. Based on national and prefecture survey data, Fujita's 1995 research clearly showed that: 1) a student's academic achievement in middle school positively correlates with his or her father's education and; 2) that a father's occupational status positively relates to the educational attainment of his children. Fujita suggests various explanations for the relationship between class difference and educational success, such as a family's earning capacity, and the possibility of teachers discriminating against lower class students. He adds though that the interpretative range of his statistical data is limited and that it does not definitively support any single explanation (1995: 133).

A number of studies have concurred that high school rank strongly correlates with college entrance (Okano and Tsuchiya 1999; Rohlen 1983; Yoneyama 1999). Rohlen's 1983 study of five high schools found that one hundred percent of boys that attended the highest rank, all-boys private high school went on to college, while only two percent of the boys at the lowest rank, city all-boys night technical high school gained entrance to a university (44). Okano and Tsuchiya's (1999: 65) national data showed that while about thirty percent of student's at academic high schools went on to do four-year university degrees, less than five percent of students at low ranked, vocational high schools did the same. Yoneyama's (1999: 34–36) data demonstrated that student aspirations and college attendance increased with the rank and prestige of the high school they attended. Her study also found that gaining entrance to the best colleges is strongly related to socioeconomic family background. 'The student population of high ranked universities, for instance, has been consistently dominated by those from the professional, managerial and entrepreneurial classes throughout the postwar years' (49).

In addition to this, Yoneyama's excellent research also revealed serious, hidden problems in the education system in Japan; problems that had worsened over time. That in Japan one's class has no bearing on one's educational opportunities is a myth propagated by the education system itself. Yoneyama's study demonstrated that the importance of socioeconomic background on educational opportunities in Japan is roughly equivalent to that in Australia. The difference being that Japanese are not as cognizant as Australians are of the fact that social class is encoded in and reproduced through its school system (50–51). Yoneyama suggests that in Japan class has been ignored as an important issue in education because the prevailing thought, particularly among educators, is that all students have an 'equal chance to do well ' (49–54). Furthermore, the meritocracy system of entrance examinations has promoted the false impression that individual effort is what produces results, regardless of the advantages and disadvantages produced by the conditions of class and/or ethnicity.

Yoneyama detailed the enormous number of strict controls imposed on students in Japanese schools and the harm that they cause. Teacher violence, she found, was widespread. For example, in just one school term, from April to October in 1985, (coincidentally, during the time of my original research), four thousand cases of corporal punishment in primary and secondary schools came to the attention of the educational authorities (1999: 96–97). Since then this number has risen, with a three-fold increase from 1985 to 1995 in the number of teachers reprimanded for physically punishing students (Okano and Tsuchiya 1999: 208–209). These figures under-represent actual teacher violence, since the number of cases not reported can be assumed to be much higher.

Increased school controls are now aimed at 'controlling the student's mind,' trying to enforce conformity in an eerie, Big Brother-type scenario. The New Course of Study, which came into force in 1993, demands that teachers give grades for students' attitudes, motivations, cooperation, responsibility and willingness to participate in various school activities. These grades are influential to the students' chances of gaining entry into a good high school (Yoneyama 1999: 10–12). Both Yoneyama (1999) and Letendre (2000) have documented the extreme number and nature of the controls imposed on Japanese school students, which range from rules about hair and school uniform regulations to prescriptions regarding behavior outside of school hours. These authoritarian methods of forcing student conformity often border on scare tactics, come at the high cost of the students' dignity and foster a sense of distrust between teacher and pupil (Yoneyama 1999: 66–75, 82–83, 126–129, 175).

Yoneyama asserts that the psychological and physical abuse of students by teachers has contributed to the alarmingly high rates of *ijime* (bullying) and *tōkōkyohi* (school phobia/refusal) in Japan (14–15, 169–177, 211–215). In effect, *ijime* is another expression of student conformity; a means by which it is enforced. For it is the students that are perceived to be in some way different (e.g., loners or those who are poor, handicapped, slow or fast to learn, or have returned from living overseas, etc.) that are bullied (168). Students who have experienced or witnessed teachers employ violence to enforce conformity turn around and do the same thing by *ijime* their weaker classmates. Another typical response is for students to simply decide that they no longer want anything to do with the education system, thus the high rates of *tōkōkyohi* (refusing to go to school).

Authoritarianism and means (coercive and psychological) of enforcing conformity in schools is striping away the last few human rights left to Japanese youth, so much so that there is little room for democracy in the state's control of education. Having presented her persuasive research findings, Yoneyama concluded:

> Thus far, I have examined non-academic aspects of school the student-teacher relationship, the question of discipline and school rules, all to do with human relations and student behavior, i.e., about socialization in the broadest sense. In this area, as we have seen, the educational systems of Japan and Australia have been heading in opposite directions—Japan, towards an increasingly autocratic and hierarchical paradigm; Australia, towards a more democratic and egalitarian paradigm...(1999: 132)

Class tracking and deviant behavior

While my study population was small, the above mentioned studies lend credence and suggest a broader relevance to my finding that class was a determining factor in gaining access to better schools. It thus seems reasonable to postulate that the streaming of students according to class, or class tracking, exists in varying degrees throughout Japan.

More relevant to this book is the relationship between class tracking in the educational system and youth deviance; a subject almost totally ignored in both the literature on education and that on youth deviance. Class tracking may begin before a child even enters kindergarten, with the wealth and status of its parents determining whether or not he or she attends an elite pre-school, that then leads to an elite elementary school, and all the way on to college. In the last chapter I demonstrated how class tracking was significant from middle school onwards; how Hoku students either attended privileged private middle schools or a local middle school with a conformist middle and upper class student population, while Minami students universally attended a local working class middle school with a bad social and academic reputation. This resulted in students from the two areas having significantly different choices and opportunities regarding which high school they might attend.

Class ecology, combined with class tracking, strongly relates to high school entrance. Nearly half of the working class youths in Minami either quit school after middle school or attended a low ranked high school. In contrast, over eighty percent of Hoku youths continued their education at a higher ranked high school. And of the Minami youths that did attend higher ranked high schools, nearly all of them were from middle, rather than lower, working class families (for more details see Chapter 4).

Family social class is the single most important factor determining what high school a student is able to enter. Academic achievement in middle school depends on home environment and educational extras such as tutors and 'cram schools.' In a single parent family or a two-parent family in which the mother works, there is little or no parental supervision of a child's study program. Lower working class families cannot afford to pay for educational extras. Added to this, the high cost of a college education (with the exception of the national universities, entrance that is the most competitive) means there is little incentive for a working class student but to just complete high school. Even if they somehow prepare themselves for college entrance examinations, their parents will be unable to afford the fees. So why bother?

Middle, and especially upper class, families have the necessary income to increase their child's chances of educational success. The mothers of upper class children are typically well educated and, not being forced to work for financial reasons, are usually available to supervise their children's homework. As seen in Hoku, family wealth also enables a child to attend expensive private middle schools that are affiliated with higher ranked high schools and colleges.

Middle school teachers recommend students for differently ranked high schools (or none at all) according to the child's grades and behavior. High schools are ranked on a *hensachi* (point order system) from low to high (see Koku Juken Annai 1999). The *hensachi* indicates the number of points (based on middle school grades and subject test results) needed to enter a given high school the higher the points the higher the rank. Students then either take an entrance exam for the particular high school they are eligible to enter or an exam for prefecture high schools. A total tally of points, based on middle school grades and high school entrance exam results, along with the teacher's recommendation (*naishinsho*) then determines whether or not a student can enter a given high school. Hence, non-conforming students (i.e., those with poor academic results, who are often in trouble at school) are recommended for low ranked high schools, while conforming students (i.e., those with middle to high academic results and no behavioral problems) are positioned to go on to higher ranked high schools.

The net effect of this ranking system is the grouping together of students with similar levels of academic achievement and pre-dispositions to conformity at the same high schools. As a result, the staff of any given high school (i.e., teachers, guidance counselors, etc.) has predetermined expectations of the academic and behavioral standards of each new in-take of students (see Coser et al 1987: 395–398; Colvin and Pauly 1988: 119–127).

Grouping all non-conforming students at low ranked high schools simply reinforces a culture of non-conformity. By definition, a student's peer group at such a school will comprise students with a similarly poor academic record, as well as those who have already been labeled as 'troublemakers.' Thus even if such a student wanted to change her or his ways it would be extremely difficult for them to do so given the prevailing atmosphere of rebellion and the peer group pressure to not even try to succeed, to passively accept one's fate. In addition to this, students of low ranked high schools are stigmatized as 'school misfits' in the wider community. Each school has it's own distinct uniform and pin, which for students from a low ranked high school acts like a 'Scarlet Letter,' signaling to the public their poor academic and social status. Such a stigma creates an expectation of trouble amongst teachers and members of the public, which makes 'deviance disavowal' extremely difficult (Schur 1971: 73). What makes matters worse is that there are no second chances after middle school. Regardless of how well a student might perform in a low ranked high school they are unable to transfer to a higher ranked school. Therefore students at low ranked high schools are given little incentive to study. They are trapped on a track that leads to manual labor or commercial-type jobs not to college entrance.

This process is inverted in higher ranked high schools. The grouping together of conforming, high academic achievers at the same high schools serves to further stimulate academic achievement and enhances conformity. The potential for non-conformity or school disobedience is minimized because students labeled as potential troublemakers (school non-conformity by poor academic achievement and often behavior troubles at middle school) are disallowed entry into the higher ranked high schools. School staff and the broader community all expect these students to do well in their studies, which are oriented towards college entrance. Given that adhering to their high school's regimented study program will determine the chances of passing college entrance examinations such students are highly motivated to conform and to strive for academic success.

In the course of my fieldwork I found that many Hoku students attended higher ranked high schools in Kaigan, considered one of the wealthier cities in Japan. Kaigan has a disproportionately large number of higher ranked high schools, a few among the best in the nation. The usual level of student homogeneity by class and conformity established through the tracking system was even higher for Hoku students attending all-boys or all-girls higher ranked high schools in Kaigan. From a social psychological point of view, the clear in-group and out-group distinctions by high school rank and area, class and behavioral (e.g., dispositions towards authority, involvement in conventional youth activities, etc.) homogeneity of students in middle and upper ranked high schools meets the criteria for bolstering group cohesion. Deutsch and Krauss stated that group cohesion depends on:

[...] social proximity, the similarity of people's attitudes and backgrounds, their common experiences of success or failure, the distinctiveness of a group or person from the other people nearby, the consonance of personalities with one another, expectations about interrelationships, and other parallels of this sort (1965: 20).

Class culture in England and Japan

As in Japan, students in England are tracked in early adolescence towards college or work depending on their school performance (Willis 1977). Those that obtain good O level test results at a middle school age go on to take A level tests, which then determine the course of their tertiary study. Students with poor O level test results are unable to take A level tests and from middle school on are put on a school curriculum geared towards commercial or blue-collar jobs.

Most English working class youths do not achieve test results that enable them to pursue courses that lead to them attending a university. Working class English youths as with their Japanese counterparts, are separated from their higher-class contemporaries at an early age. Often feeling disenfranchised by and alienated from an education system that they perceive to be designed for the upper and middle classes, working class students typically experience failure early in their school experience and this fosters an anti-school subculture. Willis (1977) provided detailed descriptions of English working class boys purposefully rejecting the middle class school system, deliberately not trying in their schoolwork and actively misbehaving.

Anti-school subcultures in both England and Japan comprise groups of defiant students who are aware that they are different from their conformist contemporaries. The similarities between the countries are underscored by two comments, one made by a rebellious secondary school student in England, the other by a defiant low ranked high school student in Japan. Talking about differences between the conformists and those in the anti-school subculture at his secondary school, the English youth said:

> I mean, what will they remember of their school life? What will they have to look back on? Sitting in a classroom, sweating their bullocks off, you know, while we've been...I mean look at the things we can look back on, fighting on the Pakis, fighting on the J.A.s [i.e. Jamaicans]. Some of the things we've done on teachers, it'll be a laff when we look back on it (Willis 1977:14).

A Japanese student I interviewed made a very similar comment.

> [...] young people study hard to enter a top university and when they are in [a university] they play [*asobi* translates as 'play' in English, though in Japanese it carries a connotation of 'letting one's hair down' or even 'getting into trouble'] to make up for the time when they were middle and high school students and studied hard and didn't play. And three years later, they enter a top enterprise...I somehow feel sorry for these young people who only think of entering a top high school, a top university, and a top enterprise. But they may be winners because they can get a steady income working for a top enterprise. Those who haven't taken this course like me can enjoy their lives for the time being. Most people play when they are in a university. But they didn't play like we did in their middle and senior high school days when most people want to play a lot. We have a lot of memories of this period and I feel sorry for those 'dark' people ... who didn't play and don't have memories of that period.

Class, high school rank and misbehavior

By the time lower working class youths reach the first year of middle school they realize not being prepared for academic success. This creates a distance between them and other more advantaged students, which encourages friendships to be formed along class lines. Their sense of alienation from the middle class values embedded in the school system becomes greater as the academic demands placed upon them increases and their inability to keep up with them becomes more evident. The response of many lower working class youths is to rebel by joining an anti-school subculture in their middle school.

Japan's education system does not recognize its class bias and instead blames the individual student for poor academic performance and non-conformity to school rules. This then provokes further rebellion and encourages such students to identify themselves with counter-school elements in the middle schools, creating an antagonistic student-school relationship.

Anti-school subcultures are dominant in low ranked high schools. Most students in these schools are from lower class families and, at least in Shonan, lived in a working class area. Conversely, academic achievement and conformity to middle class values characterizes student populations at higher ranked high schools. These students are predominantly from middle and upper class families and, at least in Kaigan, resided in middle and upper class communities.

My research found that the frequency and seriousness of a youth's self-reported acts of misbehavior was strongly related to the rank of the high school she or he attended. Other factors, such as youth-parent relations, access to play areas and so on, were relatively inconsequential compared with the influence of school rank on rates of misbehavior. Table 3.1 lists the self-reported rate of misbehavior by high school rank for Minami and Hoku students according to gender.

For males and females in both communities, misbehavior rates of students at low ranked high schools was two to three times higher than that of students at middle or high ranked high schools. Looking at with-in group percentages, nearly three times more Minami than Hoku students attended low ranked high schools, thus explaining their overall higher rate of misbehavior (4.6 to 3.5).

Gender differences regarding misbehavior are particularly noteworthy. Contrary to the common assumption that boys misbehave more than girls, Minami females have a higher average rate of misbehavior (4.8 to 4.5) than Minami males. This is largely attributable to the fact that more girls than boys attended the area's low ranked high schools (female rates were somewhat lower than males within each high school rank). Hoku males misbehaved at an average rate nearly three times (6.1 to 2.5) higher than that of Hoku females, though this difference is skewed by the large average (12.3) of acts of misbehavior reported by Hoku males at low ranked high schools. This pattern of misbehavior suggests that gender difference in misbehavior is notable among middle and upper middle class youths but not working class young people.

Gender differences are less pronounced among working class people compared with those in the middle and upper classes. In most working class families the mother works and quite often the husband and wife work together, for example, as butchers or dry cleaners, in a small family run shop. In this context, where economic necessity demands members of both genders work together, girls become more like boys and are freed from the middle class Japanese values that emphasize gender differentiation. This also finds expression in the education system, with nearly half of all the middle and upper class Hoku middle school students being sent to gender specific schools, while every Minami working class student attended the local, mixed-gender middle school.

Gender discrimination in the job market may also have a bearing on high school attendance and thus misbehavior activity. Job opportunities for high school and college graduates favor males and this places greater pressure and more emphasis on lower class boys gaining academic success than their sisters. This might partly account for the greater proportion of lower class females than males attending low ranked high schools. Even so, the stigma attached to being from the lower working class and attending a low ranked high school applies equally to males and females. Like the boys, the girls rebelled and were at least as active as them in engaging in misbehavior.

The final entry in Table 3.1 indicates the percentage of students from each class according to high school rank. As this shows, class strongly correlates with high school entrance. In Minami, nearly all or eighty-five percent of students at low ranked high schools belong to the lower-working class, while all Minami students at high ranked high schools come from the middle-working class.

Table 3.1 High school rank and misbehavior by gender and area

Misbehavior acts (avg.) by area and gender	High School Rank			Average & number
	Low	Middle	High	
Minami				
Female (n)	6.1 (8)	2.3 (3)	3 (2)	4.8 (13)
Male (n)	7.4 (5)	3.25 (8)	3.6 (5)	4.5 (18)
	6.6 (13)	3 (11)	3.4 (7)	4.6 (31)
school rank % (n)	45% (13)	32% (11)	23% (7)	
% lower working class (n)	85% (11)	18% (2)	0% (0)	
Hoku				
Female (n)	4 (4)	1.7 (14)	2.9 (15)	2.5 (33)
Male (n)	12.3 (3)	5.7 (6)	2 (4)	6.1 (13)
	7.6 (7)	2.9 (20)	2.7 (19)	3.5 (46)
school rank % (n)	15% (7)	44% (20)	41% (19)	
% upper class (n)	0% (0)	45% (9)	74% (14)	

Note: High school rank was measured by point intervals (hensachi) based on a national guide to high school ranking (see Yoder 1986). Misbehavior acts are self-reported acts of youth misbehavior up to the adult age of 20. Self-reported misbehavior acts include all acts from the original and follow-up studies, with each act counted only once. This table does not include data relating to eight Minami and six Hoku youths either because information on their misbehavior after middle school could not be obtained in the two follow-up studies or, in the cases of two Minami youths and one Hoku youth, because they were middle school graduates. In all likelihood, the misbehavior rate of Minami youths is even higher than Hoku youths than that indicated here because fewer Minami youths returned the 1st and 2nd follow-up questionnaires in which they would have recorded their acts of misbehavior during middle and/or late adolescence.

Ordinal school rank differences and class in Hoku are equally strong. Moving from low to high ranked high schools, the percent of upper class students progressively increases. Looking at the extreme categories, all Hoku students at low ranked high schools are from middle class families, while seventy-four percent of students at high ranked high schools come from upper class families (see Chapter 4 for the criteria used to measure family social class within Minami and Hoku).

Labeling by high school rank

Teachers and school officials at low ranked high schools tend to perceive and treat students as school failures and potential troublemakers. In direct contrast, at higher ranked high schools students are expected to be well-mannered, high achievers. This difference in attitude and expectation creates very different school cultures and results in divergent levels of student identification with different schools. My study showed that students at low ranked high schools had a weak attachment to school, whereas those at higher ranked schools felt positive about their school.

As the following quotes attest, students at low ranked high schools complained of overly strict school rules, teacher violence and felt a sense of shame and embarrassment about attending such stigmatized schools. A Minami boy at a low ranked high school said that there are some things he liked and other things he disliked about his school. And what did he dislike about his school? 'The teachers. There are teachers who hit students' (Yoder 1986: 155–156). A Minami girl at a low-ranked all girls' high school made these comments about why she disliked teachers in my interview with her.

Interviewer: Do you get along with the teachers at your school?
Girl: No. The school is strict which makes it harder to get along with teachers.
Interviewer: Who is strict?
Girl: Most of the teachers are strict, and they even use physical violence on us. (Yoder 1986: 156).

At another low ranked high school, a female student complained of overly strict school rules that even govern, for example, the color of the students' socks and the nature of their hair styles absolutely no perms allowed.

We are checked every morning. At the school gate, students with the weekly duty, check our fingernails or the things inside our bags. The third year student and a teacher [check us]. My friends will pass me, but serious ones [third year student checkers] will take our I.D. card away, and write "nails" in it, if we keep our fingernails long (Yoder 1986: 159–60).

Almost every student that attended a low ranked high school expressed a feeling of shame about attending such a school. They did not want others to know the name of their school for fear that they would look down on them because of the schools 'bad' reputation.

A Minami girl that had attended a low ranked high school was so ashamed of her school that even after graduation she did not want anyone to know its name. She was well aware of the stigma attached to students that attended her low ranked high school. When asked how she felt when someone asked her the name of the high school she went to she said,

> At that moment I feel like I don't want to say [its name]. I don't care if they think it's a low ranked high school but there is misbehavior at my school and others may think of my school as full of [students] misbehaving. I don' like it (Yoder 1986: 194).

School attachment at higher ranked high schools

Students at higher ranked high schools generally liked school, got along well with teachers and were proud of their school. Most mentioned that their school was not strict at all and that the teachers trusted the students. One Hoku girl's comment typifies their feelings. Asked if her school was strict, she said, '…not at all. No one obeys the regulations although there are regulations [it's] almost nothing' (Yoder 1986:175).

Asked if her school banned colored socks, she replied:

> No, they don't. Any color is fine. Well, according to the rules, we are not supposed to wear colored sweaters or sweatshirts, but everyone does. They [the teachers] don't say anything about it. It's pretty liberal [there] (Yoder 1986: 176).

Overall, the higher ranked a school, the more proud its students were of it. The following comments suggest this came about from the students' awareness that their school's high rank placed them in a privileged status position. Asked if she was proud of her high school, a Hoku student at a higher ranked high school replied:

> I'm proud of [my school]. My high school has traditionally been a high ranked school. We are good at sports, too. The name of the school is pretty well-known, so I'm not embarrassed to say its name (Yoder 1986: 177).

Another Hoku student at a higher ranked high school said, 'I'm proud of my school. I would be insulted if people made fun of my school' (Yoder 1986:178). Asked if she liked the school uniform, she replied, 'Yes I like it. Wearing the uniform strengthens our group conscious...It gives us discipline and uniformity' (Yoder 1986:178).

High school rank, school system and misbehavior

The subculture of anti-school sentiment in low ranked high schools was fueled not just by grouping together all students with a history of academic and behavioral problems, but also from their teachers' and school officials' suspicion and mistrust of them and the strict controls imposed on their behavior and appearance. It is the school system, however, not teachers, that sets the criteria which divides and channels students into differently ranked high schools, the various ranks and status of which are well understood by the public. Students at low ranked high schools are seen as academic under-achievers, troublemakers and misfits labels accorded them by the school system. They respond to this stigmatization by acting out these labels, fulfilling the adult world's negative expectations of them. As the high school rank rises, so too does the public's perception and expectation of its students' academic and behavioral performances. Students at high ranked schools tend to feel good about self because they are treated well by their school and the broader community. This in turn encourages even greater conformity and academic excellence on the student's part.

The Japanese education system is structured in such a way as to create these vastly different school cultures and the disparity between the experiences of the students in them. Competition for entry into a good high school is fierce and family income and home environment are more important factors than 'raw' academic ability in determining whether or not a student succeeds. Without private tutoring, attendance at 'cram schools,' the latest school equipment (e.g., up-to-date computers), a home environment favorable to study (which usually means an educated mother available to assist with homework), the chances of gaining entry to a good high school are extremely slim. A very small minority of lower working class Minami young people attended higher ranked high schools and a few middle-class Hoku youths entered a low ranked high school. These though were the exceptions. Simply put, the middle class value oriented hierarchical educational system works to the advantage of the higher class and to the disadvantage of the lower working class. It's disregard for class culture and differential class opportunities sets the very stage for rebellion among lower working class students while at the same time preserves the 'status quo' for higher class students. As the next two chapters illustrate, this also greatly contributed to the social reproduction of class when these adolescents became young adults.

4 Rebellion and the Transition into Early Adulthood

Youth rebellion and young adulthood

This chapter examines young people's rebellion from and conflict with the adult social control establishment during their transition from adolescence to early adulthood. My research revealed that lower working class Minami youths experienced the most conflict during adolescence, while their upper class Hoku counterparts experienced the least (see also Chapter 5). This is attributable to that the values embedded in the class culture of lower working class Minami youths are in conflict with those expressed through the dominant, national middle class culture. Disadvantaged by their lower class status position, such youths find themselves at odds with the mainstream way of life.

Youth rebellion characterized the adolescent life of lower working class Minami youth and a small minority of middle class Hoku youth, that I will call 'Hoku rebels.' Rebellion began at an early age for the lower working class Minami youths, and escalated for both groups while they attended low ranked high schools. Their non-conforming behavior as adolescents restricted their future chances of 'making it' in middle class society, leading them to a low socio-economic status as adults.

Family social class background

New information gained through the first and second follow-up studies enabled me to take into account other factors regarding the youths' family social class backgrounds and thereby establish a more finely calibrated understanding of the class divisions in the two areas. Family social class background was then measured by four class conditions: (1) parents' occupations; (2) parents' education; (3) single or dual-parent family and (4) mother's working status. Education and occupation are standard inter-correlated measures of social class. Education positively relates to occupational status and together they represent a measure of the parents' social status position in Japanese society.

While a father's education and occupation have long been standard measures of family social class in Japan, a mother's education and occupation is now considered equally important. The parents' combined educational and occupational status is a strong measure of a youth's social class background. Typically, it is the mother that spends most time with the children and it is she who is usually charged with the task of guiding their education. More highly educated mothers have higher expectations and better know how to prepare their children for academic success than less well educated mothers.

Traditionally, the ideal occupation for a mother in Japan has been that of a housewife. This has enabled her to focus on the primary task of socializing the children, in particular, attending to their educational, nutritional and social needs. With the exception of mothers with middle to high occupational status, that is, those with professional or business careers, the need for a mother to work suggests a family experiencing income pressures. And, as with a father's occupational status, the lower the mother's occupational status, the lower the family's social class.

In Japan, a strong stigma continues to attach to single-parent families. This shows itself in that only about three percent of Japanese youths live in single parent homes (Yonekawa 2001). Letendre noted that Japanese middle school teachers associate delinquent behavior with single parent families (2000: 120). This suggests children from such families are labeled as potential delinquents from an early age. Most of the youths from single-parent families are placed at an educational disadvantage because of the likelihood that only one of their parents will be involved in their education and no adult will be home to supervise their homework and to meet their other educational needs. Unless the single-parent's occupational and educational status is high, children from single parent families are considered lower class.

In Minami, there are two classes, lower and middle working class. Most of the Minami young people I interviewed (20 of 38) belonged to the lower working class. The criteria for considering a Minami adolescent to be lower working class were if they lived in a single parent family or in a two-parent family where both parents' had a high school education or less and the mother worked. Also, occupational status for lower working class parent(s) was more of a lower than middle class status such as blue collar, service oriented work, small shop workers or proprietors or working for a small business. Eighteen Minami youths came from middle working class families. They lived in two-parent families and at least one parent had a college education or both mother and father were high school graduates and the mother did not work. Also, a middle working class youth's parents' occupational status was higher than that of the parents of their lower working class counterparts.

In Hoku, a social class division existed between upper and middle class families. All but one of the fathers of the twenty-six Hoku youths from upper class families that I interviewed were college graduates (the exception being a boy from a wealthy landowning family) and the vast majority of their mothers were either college graduates or special school graduates. Also, the mothers either didn't work (which was true for twenty-four of twenty-six cases) or worked in the professions. This contrasted with the situation for the twenty-five Hoku youths from middle class families. In these families, at least one parent did not have a higher education and a greater percentage or a little more than a third (nine of twenty-five cases) of the mothers worked. Also, the occupational status of the parents in these families was lower than that of the parents in upper class families.

There were some cases in both Minami and Hoku where the parents' educational status was unknown. In these cases the father's occupation, mother's working status and the quality of the house or apartment in which they resided were used as measures of family social class.

Characteristics of youth rebellion

Youth rebellion against adult authority is signified by acts of misbehavior, trouble at school and police contact. To a lesser extent, conflict also occurs in young peoples' relationships with their parents. Such forms of conflict, however, differ in degree and kind.

Acts of misbehavior include various kinds of misconduct, some considered more seriously deviant than others. The age an adolescent first engages in such misconduct and the context in which it occurs are important to understanding the extent of the individual's non-conformity. Reading a pornographic magazine in the back of a bookstore when you are seventeen is not nearly as rebellious an act as hanging around with a youth gang when you are fourteen, yet both are considered single acts of misbehavior. Similar differences exist in youth-parent relationships, which are by nature particular and are yet a part of a class culture. Thus, a child's rebellion against her/his parents must be understood within the context of family's social class and the parent's expectations.

Similar to the last two chapters, applicable concepts and theories regarding adolescent deviant behavior will be applied to understand delinquency-prone situations. This process will now highlight the universality of youth deviance and, in particular, the role class ecology plays in it.

Adolescent deviant behavior is learned in interaction with others. Or, to put it another way, without deviant others it is unlikely that an adolescent will engage in deviant behavior. This is the core of Sutherland's (1988: 299–301) differential association theory and fits neatly with class ecology. Given the high level of youth crime in Shonan and the prevalence of anti-school attitudes and behavior in the local middle school, Minami youth are presented with ample opportunity to 'learn' deviant behavior at a young age.

Labeling theory is concerned with the branding of deviants and the debilitating effects of isolating 'deviants' from so-called 'normal' people (Coleman and Cressey 1990: 406; Liska 1987: 115–116). As detailed in the last chapter, the marking, assigning and sending of 'student misfits' to low ranked high schools is a process of deviant labeling. This is related to class ecology because it is predominantly lower class students that end up at low ranked high schools, where anti-school subcultures are well established. These anti-school subcultures exhibit many of the characteristics of Cohen's (1988: 286) notion of subculture. With status attainment blocked and ready access available to a reference group of peers sharing the same fate, further deviance almost becomes inevitable.

In order to commit certain deviant acts an adolescent requires more than learnt behavior and the desire to rebel, but also the means to carry them out (Farrell and Swiggert 1988: 296). For example, youths are prohibited from buying alcohol and cigarettes and yet smoking and drinking are two common acts of misbehavior (see Appendix 3). One reason for this is that it is easy for Japanese adolescents to illegally buy alcohol and cigarettes. Both items can be purchased from vending machines outside the entrance of liquor and tobacconist stores. So, when adults were not looking, Minami and Hoku youths easily purchased their preferred brand of cigarettes and alcohol.

Adolescence is typically a time when children conform to the demands of their peer group, often despite the opposition of their parents. This, however, does not necessarily mean that a given adolescent goes along with the peer group because they believe in the rightness of the group's ideas or actions. Linden and Hackler (1988: 353) refer to associations with a particular peer group and deviant activity as involving affective ties. Young people with weak ties to conventional society are more likely to develop associations with deviant youth. Affective ties to a deviant peer group facilitate deviant activity not out of commitment and belief in what they do but more from being outside of mainstream youth activities and seeing some value in committing deviant acts. As we will see later in this chapter, this was precisely the case for the lower working class youths in Minami and the Hoku rebels.

As with most adolescents, the lower working class youths in Minami engaged in deviant behavior with their peers. Together, they smoked in various locations throughout the neighborhood or nearby. For example, they smoked in game centers, fast food joints and on the street in the Shonan entertainment district, in the back corner of one small Minami store while the shop owner conveniently looked the other way, at a park where they could hide and lookout for adults, especially the police, and at one of their homes when the adults of the house were absent. Smoking was a group activity, an 'in-thing' to do for members of the anti-school subculture.

Misbehavior among lower working class Minami youths

Twenty (eight females and twelve males) of thirty-eight Minami youths came from lower working class families and nearly half (eight) from single-parent families. For those with a father living at home, the father's were employed in either blue-collar jobs or as employees of small commercial shops (hardware store, butchers, etc.). Very few of them were businessmen. All of their mothers worked, mostly in low status service jobs.

Lower working class children actively engaged in acts of misbehavior at a young age. Their misbehavior began in middle school and escalated after being sent to low ranked high schools.

They averaged roughly twice as many acts of misbehavior (six compared to three acts) as did their Minami middle working class and higher class Hoku contemporaries. Gender made no difference, with lower working class females misbehaving as frequently as the males. As such, they were the only class grouping for whom conflict with the adult social control establishment at school and with the police was normative. Compared with their higher class counterparts, they received far more counseling for causing trouble at school and had much more contact with the police.

Class culture

Each class expresses its own set of values, norms and beliefs through its class-culture, by the everyday activities of its 'members.' In this way, lower working class culture copes with its economic disadvantage by maintaining that 'making it' in middle class society is not particularly important. Of course, the attitudes of individual lower working class youths differ about such matters. The best way of understanding class culture is through ethnographic research. Thus, what follows is an ethnographic rendering of the 'meaning' of class culture as interpreted by the actions and opinions of the youths of Minami and Hoku. In this, and the chapters that follow, individual youths are given fictitious names to protect their anonymity.

For more than three years, I spent a lot of time in Minami and for some of that time I rented an apartment in the community. As a result I came to know where each young person lived and what was happening in the neighborhood, which families were very poor, which others were middle class. Interviews with youths usually took place in their homes, that enhanced my feel for their domestic and family lives. Class was expressed through the standard of the living facilities, the location of the dwelling, the dress, small-talk and mannerisms of family members and whoever else happened to be there at the time. While, for obvious reasons, I did not ask for tours of people's homes. Nor did I spend a long time in any one home. Still, through my many home interviews and growing acquaintance with people in Minami, I developed a good sense of their working class lives.

I found that although lower working class youths were cognizant of their social disadvantage, in a phenomenological sense, they had a different way of constructing their reality. The following vignettes present what Lofland (1986: 71–75) calls 'meanings,' which depict variations in the youths' attitudes and feelings about their lives.

Yuko lived in a low-rent apartment with her mother and older brother. Her parent's were divorced and the mother worked in an unspecified job for a small company. Yuko, her mother, brother and his girlfriend were all present when the interview began. Yuko asked for the others to leave and we sat down at a small table and, as with all the interviews, after a short while I asked if our talk could be taped – a request to which she agreed.

The setting was very informal – nobody bowed when first meeting me and soon after Yuko and I began our talk, Yuko's mother lit up a cigarette and fixed herself a mixed alcoholic drink. At first, like many of the youths, Yuko was curious why a foreigner wanted to interview her. After explaining the reasons why and showing an interest in her life, she settled down and the interview began.

Yuko was a first year high school student at a low ranked high school. She also worked part-time in a Chinese noodle shop. Throughout the interview she spoke very directly but in a low voice that was hard to hear. Yuko expressed short, to the point, negative feelings about her part-time job, school life, mother and so on. When asked if she liked working in the noodle shop she simply said '*amari*' ('not at all'). And when asked if she likes Chinese noodles she replied, '*kirai*' ('I hate [noodles]'). Regarding her school, she said, '*nanika hen*' ('there is something about it that is strange'). And when I asked which sort of teachers did she like and dislike, she said she liked teachers that '*urusakunai*' ('are not loud or bothersome') and disliked teachers that are '*urusai*' ('loud, bothersome'). In response to a question about the kind of character that *urusai* teachers have, she said, '*ijiwaru*' ('they are bullies'). And how did she feel when, on one occasion, she was scolded at school? She felt the teacher was '*urusakatta*' ('bothersome').

Etsuko lived in run-down, one-story house alongside a noisy street. Her mother worked at a sushi shop and her father was a truck driver. In very cramped quarters, she lived together with her parents, a younger brother and her grandmother. Throughout the interview, loud 'new music' blasted away in the background.

In contrast to Yuko, Etsuko had a positive view of life. She was very cheerful and was happy listening to her favorite music that was playing in the background while we talked. A third year student at the local middle school, she had fallen in love with a boy.

Everything was positive – school life, neighbors, and relations with her parents, and so on. This despite the fact that, laughing in-tune with music, she admitted that she was *ochikobore* in her studies (which roughly translates as 'a drop-out,' someone who is failing). This didn't bother her at all, as she intended to go to a low ranked public high school, one that was easy to get into.

One small incident during the interview suggested that a warm, trusting relationship existed among the family members. While Etsuko was telling me a funny story about her tomboyish ways her grandmother entered the room and gave me a cup of coffee. We were both laughing and I said to the grandmother, 'I bet she is like you.' The grandmother, ever so gently, said, 'Yes, we are alike,' and then left us alone.

Etsuko adored her father and had a friendly relation with her mother. Unlike Yuko, she was content with her working class way of life. Still, her schoolwork was poor and she was not prepared for nor oriented towards academic success. Like most of her lower working class contemporaries, she was on track to attend a low ranked high school.

Kenta was working on his motorcycle when I interviewed him in the front yard of his small house. He lived with his parents, a younger sister and his grandparents all in a small, one-story house, right in the center of Minami. His parents both worked at the same company. Kenta was on the fringes of the lower working class. Living in a two-parent family, with both parents holding down steady jobs and owning their own home, he was comparatively well-off.

Kenta was neither positive nor negative in his outlook, rather he had an apathetic attitude towards the middle class way of life. A second year high school student at a low ranked high school, he didn't belong to any school club and instead worked part-time washing dishes from five to ten in the evening. He didn't care much for school, was failing in his schoolwork and had no particular feelings about recently having been counseled at school for breaking school regulations by riding his motorcycle there. The school informed his parents about this misdeed but they were not at all angry about it.

Kenta met his best friends at school. They were all into bikes and were quite a wild bunch, with some, like him, associating with a youth motorcycle gang like *bōsōzoku*. He felt distant from adults, who he thought couldn't understand people his age because their way of thinking was so different. He was not prepared for, nor was he interested in taking, college entrance exams and he didn't seem to have any clearly defined ambitions.

Activities

By studying activities that youths engaged in we gain an under-standing of how they spent their time outside of school. Most in-school activities were organized through school clubs, though most club activities took place outside of school hours. The activities outside of school ranged from attending *juku*(private preparatory school) through to associating with a youth gang. Activities also operated as class markers, differentiating a lower working class youth from a higher-class youth. Lower working class youths were involved in non-conventional youth activities, whereas the far majority of their high-class contemporaries were very active in conventional youth activities (see Chapter 5 for more details).

The following account describes the family backgrounds and activities of lower working class Minami youths and the lives they were leading as young adults at the time of the last follow-up study. It begins with siblings and then proceeds chronologically, starting with the youngest sub-set of adolescents up to the oldest. The last sub-set of lower working class Minami youth presented is those involved with youth gangs.

Minami lower working class siblings

The adolescent lives of children from the same family usually followed a similar pattern. Involvement in activities and orientations towards school were closely tied to lower working class culture, reflecting their upbringing and associations with other lower working class youths. Two sets of siblings were part of the initial study and were traced through the follow-up studies into early adulthood.

A brother and sister named Michio and Keiko lived in the most run-down apartment building in Minami. They were the oldest of eight children, with whom, along with their parents, they shared a small, cramped apartment. Their father was a truck driver and their mother a housewife, who was busy taking care of all the children, the youngest of whom, an infant, was in her arms when I met her.

Michio was the eldest in the family and was working in a factory when we first met. A middle school graduate, he'd had no intentions to going on to high school. When he was a student, school meant nothing to him. He didn't care about the teachers or the school. During his middle school days, he, along with a number of other like-minded youths, used to ditch school and smoke and hang-out at game centers.

Michio's best friend, Seiji, lived in Minami. Seiji's parents ran a butcher's shop in Minami. Seiji, his parents and his sister lived in a small apartment at the back of the shop. He too stopped his education after middle school and got a job as a mechanic. Like Michio, he didn't like middle school and only just managed to graduate. Seiji was also active in youth crime during his middle school days and both boys were caught smoking at a game center, their offenses written up.

These two boys hung-out with a loose group of about twenty friends, all of whom were outside of mainstream, middle class Japanese society and were thought of as being *furyōshōnen* (bad kids). They smoked, drank, read porno magazines, went to bars and other places off-limits to youths, stayed out late at night, gambled (*pachinko*), were unruly, caused disturbances in public places and a few of them inhaled paint thinner and associated with a youth gang.

During the second follow-up study, after a number of visits to Michio's apartment, I was finally able to contact him. He was just leaving home and didn't have much to say. Somehow he had managed to make it through adolescence and was by then married and a father to two children. He and his family live in a small apartment, a short walk away from Minami. Michio is now some kind of businessman.

A Minami small store operator and friend of Michio's and Seiji's families told me that some years ago both boys contemplated attending a night high school but then never did. She said they remained best friends until Seiji moved out of the neighborhood. Nowadays Seiji lives about an hour's train ride north of Shonan. He is married with two children and works as a printing press operator.

When I first met Keiko she was a middle school student. Like her older brother, she didn't like school or the teachers and did poor schoolwork. Keiko hung around the 'bad kids' and saw herself as a 'bad girl.' She was right on course to attend a low ranked high school.

Like Michio, Keiko did not respond to either the first or second follow-up sets of mailed questionnaires. Michio had told me she had married after graduating from high school and, during the second follow-up study, I discovered where she had moved. Unfortunately, though, I was a little too late, as she had just moved from that neighborhood, which was not far away from Minami, to another prefecture quite a distance from Shonan. The apartment building in which she had been living was almost derelict. A young married couple that had moved into her apartment said she had lived there with a small child and husband.

Mariko and Akiko were two sisters from a single-parent family. They were very generous with their time and provided me with a good deal of information during the original research and at the time of both follow-up studies. When we first met, they were living with their mother – their father had died when they were in elementary school. The mother had less than a high school education and worked hard as a photograph processor. The eldest, Mariko, had just graduated from a low ranked high school and Akiko (see also Chapter 7) was about to enter a low ranked high school.

Neither Mariko nor Akiko had ambitions to attend a higher ranked high school or to go to college and so had a lot of free time to explore their adolescence. Typically for lower working class Minami girls, they were detached from conventional youth activities. Instead, early on in middle school, they and their best friends began misbehaving – smoking, drinking and ditching school. Akiko and a few of her girlfriends were sexually active in middle school, while Mariko began dating during her first year of high school. They both held part-time jobs when in high school and Mariko had plans to marry after high school graduation.

Akiko fitted easily into the anti-school subculture in the low ranked high school that she attended. It did not take long before she was in trouble at school. She violated the school's dress code by wearing body ornaments and was counseled for her rebellious ways. She also rode a motorcycle and was contacted by the police who suspected her of motorcycle theft. By this time, Mariko was married with a small child. Akiko hoped to follow her example after her high school graduation.

As is common in many lower working class families, Mariko and Akiko's mother did not expect her children to succeed academically. This is a key difference between lower working class and higher-class cultures, one with significant ramifications for lower working class students. The schools that both sisters attended had held similarly low expectations regarding the academic achievements of their lower working class students. The incentive to study was simply not there. As Mariko said the last time we talked, in 1999, 'there was no use going to a low ranked high school since we (students) were not being prepared for college entrance.' Like the majority of lower working class students, the sisters were oriented towards merely finishing high school. This had the effect of distancing them from the whole school experience and other conventional youth activities like social clubs and *juku*. With only a high school education their hopes for a good life centered on marriage.

Lower working class girls marry young. Mariko and Akiko both married well below the average female age for marriage in Japan, which is about twenty-six. Like her, Mariko's husband is a high school graduate. He is a truck driver and they have two children in elementary school. Akiko 'married up,' her husband being a college graduate and an engineer. She is a housewife with a four-year old daughter and was pregnant again the last time we talked at her mother's house in March 1999.

Minami lower working class middle school students

From middle school onwards, most lower working class Minami youths were not oriented towards 'middle class academic success.' This was evident among the sibling case studies and is supported by five of the six case studies of lower working class Minami middle school students.

As described earlier, Etsuko was a hip middle school student. She was into the latest pop music and was in love with her boyfriend. She didn't seem particularly conscious of her family's socio-economic disadvantage, and certainly if she was she didn't blame anyone for it. She simply saw herself as not being very smart and that it was inevitable that she would attend a low ranked high school.

Etsuko's family moved to a Shonan factory area about five kilometers from Minami. During the second follow-up study I went to their new home and met the mother. A kind person, she invited me into their small but comfortable house and we talked for more than an hour. She told me that Etsuko had married her high school sweetheart soon after graduation. Nowadays, she is a housewife with two small children and her husband is a carpenter. During our talk, Etsuko's mother said her daughter complains that her son never listens, that regardless of what she tells him to do he just goes his own way. With a grin, the mother said, 'Now Etsuko knows how I felt.'

During my initial research I met five lower working class Minami boys who were all attending the local middle school. All except one were only marginally attached to the middle school and did average to below average schoolwork. Two in particular exhibited early signs of being oriented towards a working class way of life. One of these, who was doing particularly poor schoolwork, was the eldest son in a family in which the parents ran a small hardware store in Minami. He was set to work after high school graduation for his father in the hardware store. At the time of the last follow-up study in 1999, he was married with two children and worked at his father's hardware store.

The other of these two boys, Nobuo (see also Chapter 7), came from a single-parent family and wanted to be a train driver. He did average schoolwork in middle school and managed to get into a middle-ranked high school. Still, his heart was set on driving trains and unlike most students at his high school he had no intention of going to college. Despite not liking school, he realized that any trouble during high school would hurt his chances of working for a railroad company (companies often check the backgrounds of prospective employees and ask their teachers for references) and so he stayed out of trouble and eventually graduated. Then his dream came true and in 1999 Nobuo was working as a train driver and was married with two children.

A boy named Akira was an exception among these middle school students. He lived with his mother and grandparents; his father had died in a car accident. Akira lived in one of the nicer homes in Minami. Thus, even though he was from a single-parent family, the family's finances appeared to be better than in most other lower working class households. Akira was into *kendo* (Japanese fencing), studied three to four hours after school everyday, did better than average school work in middle school and was one of the few youths that actually liked the school.

In 1999, I met Akira's grandparents at his family's home. They told me he had done well for himself, his academic achievements leading to college entrance and graduation. Akira no longer lives at home and was at that time a single businessman working and living in Tokyo. I failed to make contact with two of the original five middle school boys in the follow-up studies. I did hear though that one of them worked as a truck driver after graduating from high school and was married with one child. None of my informants knew anything about the fate of the other boy.

Minami lower working class high school students

As lower working class Minami youths entered middle adolescence their activities became increasingly rebellious. As we have seen, this was largely due to them attending low ranked high schools where anti-school subculture groups were the norm. These students were at best minimally connected to conventional, middle class youth culture.

Eriko and Natsumi were second year students at low ranked high schools when I first met them. Eriko lived in a small, run-down one-story house. Her father was a public worker employed by the city and her mother worked in a *bento* (lunch box) shop. Like most other lower working class high school students, Eriko worked part-time and did not belong to any high school club.

Eriko's schoolwork was poor and she didn't care much for her high school. Typical of students at low ranked high schools, she and her friends were non-conformists and often engaged in acts of misbehavior. Eriko and her friends went to game centers, gambled at *pachink*o parlors, dated, smoked cigarettes and drank alcohol.

It was more difficult to follow-up on lower working class youths than youths from the other sub-class groups. More lower working class families moved out of the neighborhood without notifying anyone of their new address. This partly explains why a greater number of the lower working class youths failed to respond to my subsequent inquiries. Interestingly, though, of the lower working class youths that did respond to my follow-up requests they were the kindest and most cooperative of all the respondents. In Eriko's case my inquiries literally met with a closed door, from behind which her mother shouted, 'She's married and doesn't live at home anymore.'

The other second year high school student, Natsumi (see also Chapter 7), lived with her father (her parents were separated), who ran a Chinese-type gambling parlor (*mahjong*) at their home. At the time of our first talk, her elder sister was also living there. Typically for a lower working class youth, Natsumi's misbehavior had begun at a young age. Along with her friends at middle school, she had smoked cigarettes, drunk alcohol and ditched school. From there she went to a low ranked high school and continued to engage in non-conforming youth activities. She dated, was sexually active and twice got into trouble for violating school rules. While in high school, Natsumi worked part-time in a fast food shop and did not belong to any school club.

Natsumi went to a special animal trimming school after high school graduation. After working a few years in a pet shop she got married and the last time we talked, in 1999, was living in a neighborhood near Minami, mothering a ten year old boy and a small infant.

Eiji and Hide were second year high school students at the time of the original study. Eiji attended a low ranked high school and lived in a two-parent family. His father, a high school graduate, was a businessman and his mother, who was less educated, worked in a cafeteria. Eiji went to the same Shonan low ranked high school as Natsumi and, like her, worked part-time while in high school. He didn't like the school and wasn't proud of going there. He didn't get along with his teachers and his schoolwork was below average. The school was strict. Eiji also commented that a lot of very bad students attended the school; a category to which he may himself have belonged, as he was often in trouble for regularly misbehaving.

Eiji followed the familiar lower working class pattern: his misbehavior began in middle school and escalated after he entered a low ranked high school. Before he was even in his teens he had gone to game centers and in the first year of middle school roughed up someone and read pornographic magazines. During his second and third years of middle school he ditched school, seduced girls and drank alcohol. By high school he was staying out late, smoking cigarettes and playing *pachinko*. When caught with cigarettes at high school he was given three days of school disciplinary punishment. The police also caught him stealing and on another occasion he was stopped and given a warning by the police for being on the streets late at night.

Despite his checkered past, Eiji defied all odds and went on to graduate from college. He is now married and works as a businessman.

Hide was from a single-parent family. His mother was deceased and he lived with a younger brother and his father who was a high school graduate and businessman. Hide very quickly became part of the anti-school subculture at his middle school. By age thirteen he was smoking, drinking, dating, ditching school, reading pornographic magazines and hanging-out at game centers. In high school he had his first sexual encounter, played *pachinko* and went out to bars and clubs. Like Eiji, he was caught stealing by the police and given a warning for being out late at night.

Hide, like many youths from single-parent families, matured early and enjoyed adolescent life. He wasn't a member of any high school club nor did he attend a *juku*. Instead, during his high school days, he worked as a newspaper boy, which meant waking up at four in the morning to deliver papers and then delivering evening newspapers after school. He also found time to play in a rock band.

Hide went to a middle ranked high school. He did not like the school, nor did he have close relationships with the teachers. He contemplated going to college, but that was not to be. After high school he began life as a businessman. Still single at the time of the last follow-up study, he was enjoying betting on horses at race tracks, gambling on *mahjong* and playing guitar in a rock band.

Minami lower working class high school graduates

Ken and Kouta had already graduated from high school and were working full-time when I first met them. Kouta's 's father worked in a small electronics shop and his mother worked part-time. Kouta worked in a restaurant. He was new to Minami and had attended high school at his last place of residence. During his high school days and shortly thereafter (i.e., between the ages of 16 and 18) he reportedly: smoked, drank alcohol, violated the curfew, dated, had sex, played *pachinko*, went to game centers, and frequented clubs, cabarets and other establishments off-limits to youths. My efforts to contact Kouta during the first follow-up study failed – he did not respond to the questionnaire – and by the time of the second follow-up his family had moved from Minami to an unknown address.

When I first met Ken he was working for a small company. He had graduated from a night high school, working full-time during the day while studying at night. His father worked at an electronic industrial plant and his mother worked at her father's small shop.

Ken's closest friends were old classmates from his night high school. Low ranked, night high schools are known to cater for students from the lowest rung of the socio-economic ladder. Ken said his friends were 'bad kids' who had all been in trouble with the police. They were into cars and often went out cruising. All of his friends smoked, stayed out late, went to bars, ditched school and read pornographic magazines. About half went to game centers and played *pachinko*. A few of them were sexually active.

Like nearly all of the lower working class Minami youths that attended low ranked high schools, Ken displayed rebellious behavior at a young age, an indication that he was not oriented towards, rather, rejected 'middle class academic success values.' At thirteen he read pornographic magazines, at fourteen he smoked and at fifteen he dated, ditched school and went to game centers and bars. By eighteen he was effectively working as an adult during the day while completing high school at night. He stayed out late and was sexually active.

Although by the time of the second follow-up study Ken's family had moved a short distance from Minami, I was able to find out their new address. Word of mouth spreads quickly in Minami and his parents had heard I was back in the community and were expecting me when I dropped in on a hot summer day in 1998. They are good people and we sat around for a few hours talking, not just about their son, but also about what had become a major family problem. Ken married soon after the initial study and soon after that fathered a baby boy. He and his wife later divorced and, as is not so uncommon in Japan, the family court forbade him or any of his relatives from having any contact with the boy until he was twenty years old. Ken's parents were extremely distressed at not being able to see their only grandchild. Ken, though, remarried and in 1998 he was working for a company. He and his wife, a nurse, were at that time living at his parent's home.

Minami lower working class youth and youth gangs

Three of the lower working class Minami youths that I interviewed were involved with youth gangs. The conventional, often misguided, fears of Japanese middle school teachers that youth crime inevitably leads to close involvement with juvenile delinquents was actually borne out in the cases of these three students. Middle school teachers typically believe there is a causal link between smoking and truancy and more serious defiant behavior, such as running away from home and substance abuse as the student becomes more involved with juvenile delinquents

(Letendre 2000: 138–139). Such beliefs found support in Sato's claim that deviant behavior led youths to join *bōsōzoku* groups (1991:115–116). For the *bōsōzoku* members in Sato's study, deviance began in middle school, where they smoked and ditched school with their friends, and escalated to the point that they became gang members. The three youths that I interviewed that fitted this pattern were living lives totally disconnected from mainstream adolescent culture.

When I first met Miho and Yuko (see earlier references to her in the class culture section) they had just finished first year at a low ranked, all-girls public high school in Shonan. Neither of them liked the school, which had a bad reputation. Their fellow students were generally rebellious and the teachers were extremely strict and sometimes resorted to violence. The standard of Miho and Yuko's schoolwork was poor and both girls had been in trouble at school. Miho had received counseling for smoking and Yuko for a range of bad behavior, including failing to do homework.

Both girls worked part-time after school. Miho worked at a *soba* (Japanese noodle) shop and Yuko at a *ramen* (Chinese noodle) shop. In the summer of her first year of high school, Miho also worked full-time at a beach shack – places well known for having connections with gangs. While it is not known whether or not her connection to a youth gang secured her the job at the beach shack, what I do know is that she not only associated with *bōsōzoku* but also was a member of another delinquent youth group.

At a young age, Miho showed signs indicative of a youth involved with youth gangs. Such adolescents typically begin misbehaving at a very early age, experience trouble at school and are violent towards their contemporaries. At fourteen, Miho drank, smoked, dated, went to game centers, ditched school, associated with *bōsōzoku,* and caused public disturbances. Once attending a low ranked high school, she was in trouble with the school authorities, harbored a near hatred for the school and began going to places off-limits to youths. By sixteen, (her age at the time of our talk) she was already a member of a youth gang. The last I heard of Miho, she was a high school graduate, married with a small child and residing in Tokyo.

Like Miho, Yuko engaged in acts of misbehavior at a very young age. At twelve she went to game centers and by the time she was thirteen she smoked, drank, ditched school and stayed out late at night. She was dating at fourteen and by fifteen she associated with *bōsōzoku* and planned to become a member of a youth gang. She was a rough girl, caused public disturbances and had a serious, violent altercation with someone. In a low ranked high school, she fitted in well with the anti-school subculture.

As one would expect, Yuko's best friends at high school were all non-conformists, girls that had rowdy, heated arguments with others and that regularly dated. Of her five best friends, four were sexually active, drank alcohol and went to game centers. Most (3 of the 5) ditched school, stayed out late, gambled at *pachinko* parlors and went to other places off-limits to youths. Two of them smoked and were members of a gang. One friend inhaled paint thinner.

I never found out what happened to Yuko. Her family moved from Minami some time after the initial research and even though a reliable source provided me with her new address, she never responded to my inquiries.

Kenta (see earlier references to him in the class culture section) was failing at his low ranked high school, had been counseled for riding his motorcycle to school and thought of himself as a 'bad kid.' He hung around with a wild bunch of high school friends. They were into motorbikes and cars, an interest that led to his association with youth motorcycle gang members. He and a few of his friends were also members of a delinquent youth group. All of his friends smoked, drank, stayed out late and read pornographic magazines. Some of them exhibited traits associated with youth gangs by being sexually active, going to places off-limits to youths, having violent altercations with others, causing trouble in public and carrying illegal weapons.

As with the two girls involved with youth gangs, Kenta began misbehaving as a very young adolescent. He first drank alcohol and read pornographic magazines when he was twelve. At fourteen he associated with *bōsōzoku*, became a member of a youth delinquent group and had a fight with someone in public. When fifteen he smoked, stayed out late and ran away from home. At sixteen he created a disturbance in public and had a violent fight.

I never heard from Kenta after our initial meeting. When I went to his home during the second follow-up study, his mother, speaking to me through an intercom at the front door, told me to get lost. I think, though, I may have seen him quite recently. Two young guys wearing dark sunglasses got out of a gangster-style car, with tinted windows and low body frame, and walked into his parent's house. I thought about knocking on the door but, remembering the past incident with his mother, decided to walk away.

Lower working class Minami youth/parent relations

In all three studies, youths were asked a number of control theory-type questions (see Chapter 2) about how well they got on with their parent(s). In the original study, youths were asked about their interpersonal relations with each parent, such as if their mother and father understood them, if they wanted to be like their mother or father, if their parent(s) were too strict and how close they felt to each parent. Other questions were asked about their mothers' and fathers' behavior, if their parent(s) smoked and drank at home and if they objected to them drinking, smoking or dating. Youths were asked if they would feel ashamed if their parent(s) knew they were misbehaving and whether or not a desire not to disappoint their parent(s) inhibited their misbehavior.

In both follow-up studies (the first occurring when these youth were older adolescents or young adults, the second when they were between the ages of 28 and 33), they were again asked about how well they got on with their parent(s). Then, in the second follow-up study, they were asked to recall their relationships with their parents during their adolescence.

Most lower-working class youngsters had good relations with their parent(s). This was partly due to the absence of one of the main sources of friction in youth-parent relations in higher-class families, namely, anxieties concerning academic success and parental imposition of strict study habits. Another probable reason for the lack of conflict despite that these youths did poor schoolwork, were often in trouble at school and were very active in youth crime, was that typically their parent(s) blamed themselves for their child's behavior. In their eyes, that they could not afford to provide their children with a good education and that they themselves were not high academic achievers meant they could not blame their children for exhibiting non-conforming behavior. Perhaps also many of these parents were themselves non-conforming youths when they were young and could therefore relate to their child's rebelliousness. In lower working class families there is less youth/parent conflict over poor school performance and troubles with adult authority because the parent[s] do not have middle class expectations of, or even hopes for, their children. This, then, is a clear indication of the clash between middle class and lower working class cultures and different perspectives regarding their child's school life and youth deviance.

The seven youths from single-parent families all got on well with their parent. Two youths lived with their fathers – one's father was separated and the other was a widower. In all five single-mother cases, the father died when the child was in elementary school. Forced to mature early, children from single-parent homes helped out around the house at least by the time they were in their early adolescence. They all admired their parent's hard work in keeping the family together. Three, in particular, had nothing but praise for their mothers and, at the time of the last follow-up study, had maintained very close relations with them.

Lower working class youths from two-parent families got on as well with their parents as any other youths in Minami or Hoku. Unlike their higher-class contemporaries, they were not under parental pressure to succeed academically. Estuko's very open and warm relationship with her parents was not unlike the youth/parent relationships enjoyed by other lower working class young people. Etsuko did poorly at school and had been dating boys since she was thirteen, yet her parents were very accepting of her. She said both her parents understood her well. Etsuko talked with her mother about everything. When I spoke with Etsuko she was fifteen and her mother had no objections to her dating at that age. On the contrary, her mother enjoyed reading the love letters Etsuko received from her boyfriend. Etsuko characterized her parents as young at heart; not strict at all. She said they all had fun together and she felt very close to them. Her father was a nice guy, who spoiled Etsuko. She in turn liked him so much that she wanted to be just like him when she grew up.

Minami lower working class youths as young adults

Almost all of the lower working class Minami youths that I interviewed remained in the same social class as their parents(s). What follows is a summary of their socio-economic status as young adults.

Mostly from the follow-up studies, among twenty lower working class Minami youth initially interviewed I was able to find out the completed education of sixteen among them; the four unknown cases in all likelihood did not go on to higher education (see

Appendix 1). Two were college graduates and, at the other end of the educational scale, two ended their education after middle school. Of the rest, only one went to a special school, and eleven of them were high school graduates.

There is a significant gender difference between the occupations of males and females, one reflecting the low job expectations of and opportunities for lower working class women. As early as middle school, Minami lower working class girls talked about marriage. A career was simply unthinkable, since they did not intend to gain a higher education and job opportunities for female high school graduates were very limited. Not one of the seven lower working class girls that I interviewed even attempted to develop a career and all of them got married, some right after high school graduation. All became housewives and had children that in 1999 ranged in age from small infants up to ten years old. Although information regarding their husbands' educational and occupational status was patchy, of the known cases, two of three husbands were high school graduates working in blue collar jobs. Given they married young and propinquity it is most likely that the others husband's social class status closely matched with theirs. In other words, the girls' class position has been socially reproduced; they ended up like their mothers, raising children in a lower working class family.

All of the lower working class males that I interviewed came to work in full-time blue-collar or business-related jobs. The two middle school graduates were initially employed in blue-collar work. Both are now married with two children. One resides in a small apartment near Minami, while the other moved about an hour's train ride from Shonan. Five of the other seven lower working class males are married all but one with children. One of them has divorced and recently remarried. The known occupations at the end of the second follow-up study in 1999 of the twelve lower working class males initially interviewed shows that they are the only sub-class of young adults employed in blue collar and service type of jobs. Their occupations were: truck driver, train operator, printing press operator, hardware shop clerk, and businessmen.

Outsiders

At the time of the original study, two brothers, Hiroshi and Yuji, had recently moved from living in an area with a high youth crime rate to Hoku. Both boys had already been in a lot of trouble before arriving in Hoku and I suspect their parents moved to Hoku hoping that a change of environment would reform their sons. Unfortunately, this did not occur. As recent arrivals to Hoku, and given that the family moved from the area a couple of years later, these two boys are considered 'outsiders.'

The case of Hiroshi and Yuji underlines the importance of ecology or area influence on deviant behavior. The large body of research in support of differential association theory fits well with the boys' past history of residence (Liska 1987: 75–77). Similar to Shonan and Minami, the area these boys had previously lived in had provided ample opportunity for them to engage in deviant behavior. This does not mean that living in a delinquency-prone area causes a youth to engage in youth crime, for as we will see in the next chapter Minami middle working class youths managed to avoid contact with deviant youths. Still, a young person who is predisposed towards non-conforming behavior has far greater potential to engage in youth deviant behavior if s/he is in close proximity to other deviant youths.

Unlike lower working class Minami youths, however, Hiroshi and Yuji came from a middle class family. Their mother was a housewife and their father, a college graduate, worked as a public employee. As will be demonstrated in a more detailed discussion later, class is not the only factor that shapes youth behavior. Class conditions dramatically influence the chances a young person has of succeeding academically and of becoming involved in mainstream youth activities, but they do not guarantee that a child will act in a conforming or non-conforming manner.

Simply moving away from a delinquency-prone environment will not necessarily deter a youth from misbehaving if he or she has a history of delinquent behavior. Delinquency control programs that involve the relocation of a juvenile offender demonstrate that even under the most controlled circumstances (placement within a conventional peer group, rewarding of conventional behavior, etc.) that the most that can be claimed for such programs is that the effects of relocation are better than those of incarceration (Kassebaum 1974: 130–140). Hiroshi and Yuji had established patterns of deviant youth behavior prior to moving to Hoku, so much so that the more conforming environs of Hoku had no impact on their behavior (also see Yuji Daida in Chapter 7).

The younger brother, Yuji, became involved in youth crime at a young age and claimed to have committed thirteen acts of misbehavior between the ages of fourteen and sixteen. He belonged to *bōsōzoku* and along with other gang members led a wild life. They smoked, drank, inhaled paint thinner, threatened and assaulted other youths, had numerous sexual relations, gambled and went out to bars and other places off-limits to youths.

Before coming to Hoku, Yuji had been arrested by the police for *bōsōzoku* activities and was expelled from a low ranked high school for assaulting his physical education teacher. He justified his attack by saying that this teacher used violence against the students, including him, so he repaid him in kind. Frequently changing jobs, Yuji was working as a waiter in a pub/restaurant when we first met.

His elder brother, Hiroshi, attended a low ranked high school before coming to Hoku. This high school had a bad reputation; even the newspaper had reported on its student troubles. Hiroshi began misbehaving in middle school: smoking, reading pornographic magazines and staying out late. In high school, his misbehavior escalated to include playing *pachinko*, drinking at bars and going to other places off-limits to youths. Hiroshi, too, had been in trouble with the police prior to the family's move to Hoku. He had been written-up and given guidance for violating the curfew and arrested for bicycle theft.

Unlike the parent's of the lower working class Minami youths, Hiroshi and Yuji's parents had middle class expectations regarding their behavior and academic achievement. Although Yuji felt remorse for all the trouble he had caused his parents, it did not deter his misbehavior. Hiroshi had a reasonable relationship with his mother but did not get on at all well with his father. He did not like his father, had no respect for him and did not want to become like him.

During his short stay in Hoku, Yuji continued to get in trouble with the law. He said the police kept him under surveillance and frequently patrolled near his home. His family soon tired of this kind of pressure and moved out of Hoku. He had a long juvenile police arrest record, which included being arrested for threats involving bribery and assault. After leaving Hoku, Yuji frequently changed jobs, married and then divorced. In 1999 he was working in a dubious job as an outdoor salesman; such work often involves soliciting near train stations and could very well involve shady activities like luring inebriated men to enter a cabaret or club and so on.

Hiroshi was not as rebellious as his younger brother was and when we first met he was studying to become a barber. He later became a barber, married a nurse, and, in 1999, they had one child and his wife was pregnant with a second.

Hoku rebels

Six Hoku middle class youths stood out from all the other Hoku adolescents because of their troubled school lives. One ended her education after middle school and the other five attended low ranked high schools. Compared to their Hoku peers, they experienced far more conflict at school and in life generally, from adolescence through to early adulthood.

By Hoku standards, Yuki came from a different family background. Both her parents were high school graduates, employed by the social welfare office, and both were deaf. Yuki was their oldest daughter. She didn't like middle school and decided not to go on to high school. Very mature for her age, at fourteen she smoked, stayed out late, ditched school and joined a youth gang. Having just managed to graduate from middle school, she began working in a restaurant.

All the fathers of the other five (four girls and one boy) Hoku rebels were businessmen and four of the mothers had middle class jobs such as department store clerks or research assistants. All the Hoku rebels attended low ranked high schools and did not get on well with their teachers. None of them liked or were proud of their school and all feared or at least did not want other people finding out which school they attended. The stigma attached to attending a low ranked high school was much worse for them than for Minami youths, because nearly all of their Hoku contemporaries attended higher ranked high schools. Considered 'school failures' in an academically successful community, they felt embarrassed and degraded. One of the girls expressed feelings common to the others.

Interviewer: If someone asks you about the school you are going to how do you feel?

Girl: At first I don't mention the name of my school. I would say I'm going to a school in [she gives the name of a city].

Interviewer: Oh, really?

Girl: I don't want people to ask about my school.

Interviewer: Why? Do Hoku neighbors ask you often [about your school]?

Girl: Yes they do. They ask me: "What school do you go to?" or something like that. Our school is rather famous for its volleyball team and they can guess the [school's] name when I tell them I go to school in [she gives the name of a city].

Interviewer: Why are you ashamed of the school when the neighbors ask you about it? Is it because other Hoku youths go to better schools than yours [she had mentioned this earlier]?

Girl: Well, as I told you before, my school is not high level, and other youth around here go to prefecture schools like [Kaigan High School] or others of a high rank. Very few youths go to [low ranked] private schools ... Everybody goes to a [high ranked] public high school while only I am going to a [low ranked] private school. I feel it's a shame to say I go to a [low ranked] private school, but if my school was of a higher rank things might be different (Yoder 1986: 161).

At the time of the original interviews three Hoku girls were attending low ranked high schools and another had recently graduated from one and was now studying at a fashion school. All complained of very strict school rules. School regulations and inspections were more like the military than what one would expect in a high school. Rigorous checks were regularly made to ensure that students' fingernails were clipped, that their hair was the proper length and had not been permed, that their school uniforms were cut to the prescribed length and were worn appropriately and that only school-specified items were brought into school.

One girl at a low ranked all-girls high school hated her teachers because of their violence against students.

Well, a male teacher slaps, pulls hair, hits the students with some objects or uses abusive language to them in a dirty way, even verbally abusing their parents. And this is done only because of the student's appearance (Yoder 1986: 194).

Three of the four girls I spoke with had violated school 'hair regulations.' One was scolded for having her hair too long, while the other two had violated school rules banning 'hair permanents.' One received school counseling and was ordered to get her hair straightened. The other girl was more cunning when the teachers questioned her about her curly hair, as she explained:

> In my case, I showed them a picture of me in my childhood when I had a hair permanent. They believed I had a natural curl [though I don't], so there was no problem. When other students are found [to have a hair permanent] they may be suspended [from school], or scolded severely and assigned some cleaning job (Yoder 1986: 201).

These girls exhibited more daring and rebellious behavior than did female Hoku students at higher ranked high schools. All dated boys, three of the four hung-out at game centers, drank alcohol and stayed out late, one read pornographic magazines and another had caused a public disturbance. One of them exhibited particularly deviant behavior for a Hoku girl, though she was not born in Hoku and attended an all-girls high school outside of the prefecture. At thirteen and fourteen years of age she: ditched school, smoked, drank, violated the curfew, dated and hung out at game centers. Then between the ages of fifteen and seventeen she played *pachinko*, went drinking at bars and clubs and had sex.

The only boy among them, Satoshi, also went to a low ranked high school and, of all the youths surveyed for this research, he reported the highest number of youth crimes. Satoshi reported seventeen acts of misbehavior, which accounts for just about every official youth crime (see Appendix 3 for a list of official acts of misbehavior). Most of his misbehavior occurred during his high school days. Except for playing *pachinko* when only thirteen, all his other youth crimes were committed between the ages of fourteen and seventeen. Along with other boys from his high school, Satoshi smoked, drank, inhaled paint thinner and ditched school. He ran away from home, stayed out late and threatened to, and actually did, assault others. He read pornographic magazines, was sexually mischievous and had sex. Satoshi played *pachinko* and frequented bars and pubs. He associated with and was a member of a youth gang. And, as one would expect, he was constantly in trouble at school and was counseled numerous times for violation of school rules and had twice been suspended.

These six middle class Hoku youths were indeed rebels. Despite the socio-economic advantages of their class and the class ecology of the suburb in which they resided, their poor academic achievements and deviant adolescent lifestyles were more akin to those of lower working class Minami youths than their Hoku peers. Low academic achievement and early signs of non-conformity resulted in one of them not going to high school at all and the others being sent to low ranked high schools. Like most students at such schools, they too, despite their class background, joined in the dominant anti-school subculture.

Activities of Hoku rebels

Unlike all other Hoku youth, the Hoku rebels were barely involved in conventional middle class youth activities. Only one of the girls belonged to a mainstream youth group, her high school cooking club. Unlike the vast majority of Hoku youth, half of the rebels worked while still being, or young enough to be, at high school. After graduating from middle school, Yuki was employed as a helper in a restaurant and two of the others worked part-time in restaurants while still studying at high school.

Unlike their Hoku contemporaries, the rebels were not consumed by the task of preparing for entrance into college. Only Satoshi intended to go to college and he didn't seriously begin to prepare for college entrance exams until after high school graduation, when he spent a year at a private college preparatory school. This, along with their generally non-participation in school clubs, left them with more free time to explore more deviant sources of fun than those indulged in by other Hoku youths.

Unconventionality was the trademark of Hoku rebels. Yuki had only one close friend, an adult that worked in a bar. They went shopping together and sometimes to the movies, but she was basically a loner and usually stayed home by herself when she had free time. In contrast, Satoshi enjoyed the nightlife with his close friends. Although underage, they went out drinking and frequented classy discotheques in Tokyo. One of the rebellious girls was into rock concerts and another girl often hung-out with her two closest friends at a hip area outside of Kaigan. Another girl was into fashion and after high school attended a special school of fashion. Only one of the girls took part in conventional Hoku youth fun activities. She did not make friends with other girls at her low-ranked all girls' high school and her only close friend was a girl she had met in her local middle school. They talked a lot together, went to movies and walked around Kaigan.

Hoku rebel youth/parent relations

Generally speaking, the Hoku rebels' home lives were less troubled than their school lives. Still, Satoshi's problems at school certainly created a strain in his relationship with his parents. He felt sorry for his parents, particularly that they had had to go to the school Principal's office on so many occasions due to his frequent violations of school rules. He liked his parents, though, and despite his more universal problem with adult authority, enjoyed a close relationship with them.

The five girls all got on well with their parents, though one complained that her parents were old fashioned in their ways of thinking. By all measures, the quality and type of relationship that the rebels had with their parents was no different from the youth/ parent relationships of other Hoku youths. The conflict they experienced during adolescence stemmed solely from them attending a low ranked high school, which effectively branded them 'school failures' in the context of Hoku's reputation for high academic achievement.

Hoku rebels as young adults

Yuki stayed out of trouble after middle school graduation. She worked at a few restaurants before getting married. The last time we talked, in 1999, she was married with two small children. Her husband was a cook in a hospital and she worked part-time in a souvenir shop. The three girls that attended low ranked high schools finished their education after high school and all took jobs as office ladies. By 1999, all three were married. One was a housewife with two children, while the other two continued to work; one even though she has a small child. The oldest rebel, the one that was attending a fashion school at the time of the first study, went on to graduate from the school and worked as a fashion designer. She was single at the time of the first follow-up study, then moved from Hoku without leaving a forwarding address, so I know nothing more about her fate.

Satoshi failed college entrance exams, spent a year as a *ronin* (students that study after failing college entrance exams) and then finally gained entrance to a college. He married his college sweetheart and they moved far away, to Hokkaido. By 1999 they had had two children and Satoshi was working as a businessman.

The last I heard, he was planning to move closer to home and work on the main island of Honshu.

Theoretical concerns

Returning to the theoretical concerns mentioned at the beginning of this chapter, the above snapshots of their adolescent lives show that class ecology is a significant factor in the deviant behavior for Minami lower working class youth. Living in a working class area, in a class culture that does not emphasize middle class values such as academic achievement and with ready access to other youth deviants, meant that a lower working class youth from Minami was much more likely to commit youth crimes. We also saw that 'outsiders' living in an area (before moving to Hoku) known for juvenile delinquency actively engaged in acts of misbehavior. Furthermore, Hoku rebels exhibited early signs of non-conformity (mainly poor schoolwork) and were sent to low ranked high schools. Excepting Yuki who ended her education after middle school, the rest were exposed to an anti-school subculture at their low ranked high schools and escalated in their deviant behavior. In accordance with differential association theory, their non-conforming behavior developed as they became acquainted with other youth deviants. Still, it remains important to try to understand how such youths ended up in that situation to begin with.

In short, class made a significant difference in the chances of a young person's exposure to the delinquent behavior of others. From at least as early as middle school, lower working class Minami youths were not oriented towards academic success. Supporting the claims of reference group theory, future middle class status attainment was more or less blocked for these youths. Their reaction to this was to form or join in with an anti-school subculture in middle school and to rebel with their lower working class peers.

Labeling theory is also affirmed in the way student misfits were directed to and isolated at low ranked high schools. As discussed in the previous chapter, class tracking of students had the obvious effect of reinforcing the negative labeling and stigma associated with attending a low ranked high school by grouping all non-conforming students in such schools. This, then, reduced the students' motivation for studying, fostered their desire for rebellion and escalated their involvement in youth crime.

The circumstances that led Minami youths to associate with youth gangs or groups of delinquent youths have parallels to those discussed in the literature on youth gangs in the U.S. (Adams 1980; Kassebaum 1974; Suttles 1968) and are very similar to those described in Greenfield's (1994) fieldwork on *bōsōzoku* in Japan. Such adolescents became active in youth crime at an early age, demonstrated tendencies towards violent behavior, were estranged from conventional youth activities and had easy access to gang membership by virtue of residence or, in the case of Satoshi, through his attendance at a low ranked high school.

Social control theory's notion that close youth-parent attachment acts as a deterrent to deviant youth behavior was not at all borne out by this study. Regardless of how active they were in youth crime, most of the adolescents interviewed got on well with their parent(s) and whether they did or did not get along with their parents had little if any effect on them becoming involved in acts of misbehavior. Though my study population was small, my findings certainly demand that two popular explanations for youth deviance in Japan – i.e., blaming the mother for the child's deviant behavior and child neglect in single-parent families – be reconsidered (Foljanty-Jost 2000a, 2000b; Hood 2001; Hoshino 1983; Letendre 2000; Schreiber 1997).

Lower class parent(s) did not expect their children to do well academically and therefore put little or no pressure on them to achieve in school. Such parents were aware that they could not afford to provide educational extras such as *juku* or a home tutor and that they were often not home to supervise their children's study or that if they were their own low level of education was not much assistance. When their children got into trouble at school or with the police they either took the blame themselves or did not think much of it. Also, as the next chapter demonstrates, the main source of youth-parent conflict is parental expectations of and pressure on their children to succeed academically – a dynamic that generally does not occur in lower working class families.

The only tenet of social control theory that related to youth deviance in this study was the non-involvement of lower working class adolescents in mainstream youth activities. Even so, the more important question is why did they not get involved. The main answer was economic. Simply, lower working class Minami youths either worked full-time after graduating from middle school or part-time while attending high school. Either way, they rarely had the time or the inclination to join a school or social club. Slightly different were the Hoku rebels, who were so detached from their low ranked high schools that they saw no need to join a school club. Detachment from conventional youth activities was a barrier to socialization towards youth conformity.

The process of transition from adolescence to early adulthood and how this relates to the social reproduction of class is discussed in Chapter 6. For now, suffice it to say that class tracking in the education system played a dominant role in determining the future socioeconomic status of these youths. Now, though, in the next chapter, we must focus on quite a different story, that of the conformity of higher-class youths.

5 Conformity and Transition into Early Adulthood

Class ecology and conformity

A common perception of Japan is one of conformity. Whether in regard to Japanese companies or crime controls, conformity has, particularly by foreign researchers, been emphasized as a way of explaining Japanese behavior. Portrayed as a unique national and/ or ethnic trait, conformity has been equated with harmony in interpersonal relationships, uniformity, collectivism, family, group and community solidarity, deference to authority, vertical reciprocal relationships, the need to belong and dependency on others (Condon 1984; DeVos and Wagatsuma 1984; Kanazawa and Miller 2000; Lebra 1976; Nakane 1970; Vogel 1980). Lost in this maze of homogeneous togetherness has been the important role class plays in maintaining social conformity. A central aim of this book is to redress this oversight.

Sugimoto (2003) has detailed the careful attention paid to pressure put on Japanese to abide by what amounts to authoritarian, state-directed rules of conduct. Social controls in Japan are intrusive and all encompassing. They range from surveillance activities within small groups such as *chōnaikai*, visible displays of power such as the *kōban* (police box) through to subtle psychological controls (e.g., government screening of school textbooks) and moralizing ideational constraints (Sugimoto 2003: 271–284). Calling this 'friendly authoritarianism,' Sugimoto argued that non-conformity and unanticipated outcomes are to be expected in the face of controls aimed at creating uniformity, homogeneity and unquestioning allegiance to one's superiors in a society as diverse as Japan (2003: 271).

Class, gender and minority group disadvantages receive scant attention in mainstream accounts of Japanese society. That such differences impede some groups and individuals to integrate and succeed in Japanese society is seldom acknowledged, since the discriminatory, hierarchical nature of the country's social controls are not a subject of debate. On the contrary, the establishment successfully promotes an 'ideology of egalitarian competition,' something often thought to be characteristic of Japanese society (Sugimoto 2003: 281–283). The 'winners' in Japanese society think they have won a fair competition, while the 'losers' are generally unaware that structural inequalities may have contributed to their failure to succeed. Sugimoto aptly observed that 'the Japanese experience appears to demonstrate that the ideology of equality of opportunity justifies the reality of the inequality of outcomes more plausibly than does the doctrine which rationalizes inequality of opportunity' (2003: 283)

Previous chapters have described the discriminatory application of social controls within the Minami and Hoku communities, particularly the schools, and young peoples' reactions to it. Youth non-conformity is class related. As I have already demonstrated, non-conformity is an outcome of a hierarchically structured educational system, one in which class tracking results in students from the same class being grouped together in ranked high schools, which replicates and reinforces class differences. The last chapter highlighted the class culture of lower working class Minami youths and its antagonistic relationship with the adult social control establishment. In transition to early adulthood, non-conformity equated with a social reproduction of class for Minami lower working class youths and downward social mobility for Hoku rebels.

In this chapter I will show how conformity to adult standards of youth behavior is a middle class phenomenon, one tied in with family social class and, for Hoku youths, local class privileges. This is not a unique finding and has parallels with Willis's (1977) work on class culture and conformity among English working and middle class adolescents and fits in quite well with a more universal notion of class differences and behavior (Henslin 2002: 153–203).

It was also demonstrated in the previous chapter that social control theory's notion that the degree of youth-parent attachment significantly influences a youth's propensity for non-conformity was not at all supported by the experiences of the lower working class Minami youths and the Hoku rebels. It also seems that variable youth-parent attachment has little effect on the conformity of higher-class youths. More concisely, the findings of this study show that youth-parent relations do not differ significantly by class, yet propensity for non-conformity does. Detailed in this chapter, largely as a result of class privileges and channeling effects of high school rank based on demonstrated conformity, school attachment was a stronger deterrent to misbehavior than close youth-parent relations for students at higher ranked high schools.

Social control theory is, however, applicable to the youths' participation in conventional adolescent activities. Whereas lower working class Minami youths and the Hoku rebels avoided conventional youth activities, as we will see below, middle and upper class youths were heavily involved in such activities. This involvement facilitated and reinforced their conformity. Liska writes,

> People involved in conventional activities simply have little time available for deviant activities. For example, an adolescent's day occupied with school activities, sports, adult-sponsored recreation, and homework leaves little time for delinquency (1987:71).

Class ecology also has a profound influence on the conformity or non-conformity of higher-class youth. While gender is not influential to the conformity of middle working class Minami youths, it is for middle and upper class Hoku youths. The more privileged family and area class conditions of Hoku adolescents meant that a little less than half of them attended higher ranked private all-girls or all-boys middle schools, compared to the Minami middle working class youths, who all attended the local Minami middle school. For these Hoku youths, gender separation continued throughout their adolescence, with the females of this grouping being primed in the conservative practices of middle class 'female etiquette.' These girls, then, represented by far the most conservative of all gender sub-groups and were noticeably more conforming than their male counterparts. Finally, reflecting broader, city class differences, most middle working class Minami students were sent to higher ranked high schools outside of Shonan, while most Hoku students attended higher ranked high schools in Kaigan.

Middle working class Minami youth

All middle working class Minami adolescents came from two-parent families. Parents' known education showed that among their fathers, one graduated from medical school, six were college graduates, two had completed some college and two were high school graduates. Of their mothers, five were college graduates, one graduated from a special school and three were high school graduates. Fourteen of eighteen fathers were businessmen, with the other four's employment being: medical doctor, architect, employed at an American military base and government employee. And, while nearly all the mothers of lower working class Minami adolescents worked in low status jobs, nine of the eighteen mothers of middle working class adolescents were housewives. Furthermore, middle working class mothers held higher status jobs than did lower working class mothers. For example, one of them was a magazine editor and another was a teacher at an elementary school.

In comparison to their lower working class peers, adolescent life and the transition to early adulthood was far less tumultuous for these eighteen middle working class Minami youths. Most of these youths were conformists at school; they received good grades for their schoolwork and belonged to school clubs. They did not exhibit high rates of misbehavior and none of them had a police record. All but two went to higher ranked high schools and not one of them was counseled and/or punished for violating school rules. From the time of middle school onwards, they hung around with other middle working class kids. Once in high school, friendships were made outside of Minami with the middle and even upper class youths that attended the same higher ranked high schools. As young adults, they now belong to a significantly higher social class than that attained by their lower working class Minami contemporaries.

Four Minami middle working class adolescents were attending the local middle school when I first interviewed them. They were aware that student-teacher conflict and student misbehavior was occurring in the school and were not proud of the school. All but one kept out of trouble, keeping their distance from the 'bad kids' and associated with the conformists that were studying hard for entrance into a higher ranked high school. The story of one child that got caught up in the turmoil at the local middle school says a lot about higher ranked high schools and Minami.

This boy became involved in the middle school anti-school subculture, but then became a conformist once he entered a middle-ranked high school. As a middle school student he had smoked, drunk alcohol and read pornographic magazines. Then, upon entering a middle-ranked high school, he changed his friends and his ways. As he said: 'When I was in middle school I used to play truant from school, stay out late, play at game centers and be mischievous with my friends. I just wandered around a lot but now I don't' (Yoder 1986: 164).

Coming from a middle class background, all four of these middle school students were oriented to academic success, did above average schoolwork and went on to higher ranked high schools. The influence of high school rank was quite evident in the self-reported misbehavior of middle working class Minami youth. With all but two having attended a higher ranked high school, eighteen middle working class Minami youths reported a low average of three acts of misbehavior, ranging from zero to ten acts.

In contrast to Hoku, in Minami a youth's gender made no difference to their rate of misbehavior. As with lower working class girls from Minami, the pattern and average rate of misbehavior for Minami middle working class girls was the same as that for the boys. This contradicts the widely held assumption that boys commit more youth crimes than girls and juvenile delinquent arrest rates have consistently been much higher for males than females. Perhaps this has something to do with that gender differences are less marked in working class communities than in conventional middle class communities. The traditional female role of housewife that is prevalent in Hoku was not in evidence in Minami. Shown in the last chapter, all lower working class Minami mothers worked and among middle working class Minami mothers' even fifty percent of them worked.

Minami middle working class youths misbehaved half as often as their lower working class counterparts and they engaged in misbehavior at an older age. Their two most frequently reported acts of misbehavior were drinking (61%) and frequenting a drinking establishment (39%). They committed these acts between the ages of fourteen and eighteen, with most of them beginning such behavior at age sixteen or older. Twice as many lower working class youths smoked than did middle working class youths. The biggest difference, though, was in the more adult and rebellious types of misbehavior. While five lower working class youths were sexually active, four of them under the age of eighteen (eighteen being the legal age for sexual intercourse), only one middle working class girl (and she at the age of eighteen) had had a sexual experience. Finally, while three lower working class youth were involved with a youth gang not one middle working class youth was.

Minami middle working class students had positive experiences of high school. Seven attended upper ranked high schools, nine went to middle ranked high schools and only two attended low ranked high schools. All these youths were conformists, they were active in school clubs, they adhered to school rules and regulations and none of them mentioned having ever been in trouble at school. Compared to Minami lower working class students, middle working class students expressed a greater liking for school, had better relationships with their teachers and experienced greater academic success. They were also proud of their higher ranked high schools. Furthermore, ten of eighteen of them went to schools outside of Shonan, which had the effect of distancing them from Minami and the culture of youth crime among Shonan adolescents.

For middle working class Minami students gaining entrance to a high ranked high school represented their first time to be amongst students predominantly from middle and upper class families. Having successfully steered clear of all of the conflict in their local middle school, they were now in a school environment where conformity to middle class school rules and standards was the norm. Also, unlike their middle school experience, they were now no longer the top achievers in the school. Still, they generally managed to do average schoolwork. A few of them said they didn't feel comfortable or didn't quite fit in with the privileged student population at the higher ranked high school. Yet, as students at such high schools they were being prepared for college entrance exams and steered towards a middle class way of life that a later college education would accord.

Activities of Minami middle working class youths

Unlike their lower working class contemporaries, Minami middle working class adolescents actively participated in conventional middle class youth activities. From middle school onwards, nearly all of them belonged to school clubs; sporting clubs being the most popular, e.g., handball, basketball, soccer, swimming, softball, soft-tennis, judo and *kendo* (Japanese fencing). Reflecting the higher rank of their schools, three were members of school music clubs, two belonged to academic school clubs and one boy was a member of his school's student organization. Two girls belonged to very conventional adult supervised adolescent clubs and had been Girl Scouts since elementary school, while another girl had pen pals in foreign countries. Another girl practiced the piano every day and one of the boys visited cultural museums with his friends.

As school conformists, Minami middle working class students not only belonged to school clubs but they were also busy studying to get into a good high school and then after that preparing for college entrance examinations. Unlike lower working class Minami secondary school students, whose tight family finances required that they work part-time while studying, the greater economic security of the middle working class students enabled them to participate in conventional youth activities and to study at home and/or *juku* in preparation for college examinations. At the time of the original study, not one Minami middle working class high school student was working part-time.

Akira and Megumi

The following vignettes create a composite picture of adolescent life for middle working class Minami youths. The family background, adolescent lifestyle and adult social economic status of Akira and Megumi are reasonably representative for middle working class Minami youths.

Akira was a middle school student when we first met. He lived at home with his parents, an elder sister and grandmother. His father, a college graduate, was a businessman and his mother, a special school graduate, sometimes worked part-time but was usually at home. He was well aware of all the troubles at the local middle school and said it was not a good school. He associated with other middle working class students and the only mischievous thing they did was play at game centers. Akira was a member of the middle school Basketball Club and did above average schoolwork. He went on to attend a middle ranked high school outside of Shonan, a school that he really liked. He said his teachers were easy to talk to and he was proud of the school, that he thought was a 'really good' school. He received average grades, reported no misbehavior as a high school student and did not even date. Akira eventually attended and graduated from college. At the time of our last contact in 1998, he was single and worked in a bank.

When I first met Megumi she was a third year high school student at an upper ranked public high school. Both her parents are college graduates. Megumi's father was a businessman and her mother was a housewife. Megumi was a member of the high school Handball

Club. She was herself a good player and her team made it to the final eight in the prefecture tournament. As with many Minami middle working class students at higher ranked high schools, she was not a top school achiever, as she had been in middle school, for she was now competing with students from very privileged family backgrounds. Her schoolwork was a little below average, mainly, she said, because she didn't study very much. Still, she liked the school and was proud of it. Like most Minami middle working class youths, she did not work part-time and was free to prepare for college entrance exams.

Megumi and her friends were strong conformists. None of them had ever engaged in any misbehavior and, like Megumi, most had not been to a game center or dated. This did not mean Megumi simply agreed with and went along with the status quo. She had her own opinions and, for example, thought that teachers were not flexible enough in handling students or that the police were concerned only with catching youths doing something wrong and ignored the circumstances surrounding the crime and the youth offender. Her individuality found greater expression when an adult. Megumi went on to lead an interesting life.

After high school graduation, Megumi went to and graduated from college. She then met and later married a man from Holland. At the time of the last follow-up study, she was living in Holland with her husband and their two children. Her husband is an architect and she works part-time as an interior designer.

Youth/parent relations among Minami middle working class youths

Most middle working class Minami youths had good relations with their parents, though no better than those enjoyed by their lower working class peers. The crucial difference between the youth/parent relations of these class sub-groups was that the middle working class parents pressured their children to study hard in order to succeed academically. This led to a few of the youths quarreling with their parents regarding their strictness, particularly in the imposition of onerous study habits.

In contrast to the experiences of the lower working class youths, some middle working class adolescents implied that their school life was better than their home life. Despite this, conflict at home did not lead to misbehavior. For example, Fumiko did not get along well with her parents, yet this did not result in her wanting to rebel and misbehave, partly because she really liked her high school (see also the upper class Hoku females below). Fumiko was very attached to her school and, like her classmates, was a conformist. This attachment and identification inhibited her from actively rebelling against adult authority. Her situation again suggests the overwhelming influence of school atmosphere on identity and misbehavior.

After graduating from the local Minami middle school, Fumiko attended an upper ranked private all-girls high school, one affiliated with a very good university located outside of Shonan. Her colleagues at the high school generally came from privileged families and represented a stark contrast to Minami adolescents. I suspect that in making friends at this school, in identifying with its elitist ethos, Fumiko felt some sense of shame about Minami and compared to other students her own less well off family background contributing to conflict between her and her parents.

Fumiko's high school was not at all strict. She had good relationships with the teachers and was extremely proud of the school, so much so that later, in the follow-up studies, she said that the best time of her life was when she was a student there. Fumiko did good schoolwork and like other students at the school stayed out of trouble. She reported no misbehavior when she was attending the school. At the time of the first follow-up study she was a college student and reported that she drank alcohol and had sometimes played truant when she was sixteen. Like most college students, she started going to pubs and taverns once she turned eighteen.

For Fumiko, life at home was very different from life at school. As a high school student, Fumiko complained that her parents were too strict. Even later, when a college student, she again objected to her parents strictness. They got upset if she came home even thirty minutes late from school, even though her college was in Tokyo, quite a distance from Minami.

When a high school student, Fumiko said her mother didn't understand her and that she did not want to become like her because their way of thinking was very different. In her opinion, her father was not much better, besides which, she hardly ever saw him.

Fumiko was one of the few adolescents that responded in the negative to two questions that, according to social control theorists, are solid indicants of the youth/parent bond deterring youths from engaging in deviant behavior. A major postulate of social control theory is that youths do not act on their desires to smoke, drink, have sex, etc., because, one, they would feel ashamed if their parents knew about it and, two, because they do not want to disappoint their parents. Asked if she would feel ashamed if her parents knew she was doing something wrong, Fumiko replied, 'Not at all.' And, asked if a feeling that her parents would be disappointed in her if she misbehaved inhibited her from misbehaving, Fumiko replied, 'As for my parents, I don't think so.' Asked, why then doesn't she misbehave, she said, 'Because I don't want to; it is not on account of my parents.'

Middle working class Minami young adults

That high school entrance is a facilitator in the social reproduction of class was clearly expressed in the young adult lives of middle working class adolescents. With the exception of two, all of these youths went to higher ranked high schools and all but one that graduated from a higher ranked high school also graduated from college. Even the two students that attended low ranked high schools went on to special schools. These middle working class adolescents became far and away the most successful young adults from Minami and, at the time of the final follow-up study were all leading very middle class lives.

All girls from middle working class families were married, two with children. Two were career women: one a middle school teacher, the other, despite being a mother, an employee of a large, well-known Japanese company. As already mentioned, one married a Dutchman and now lives in Holland and has two children. She is a part-time interior designer and her husband is an architect. One middle working class Minami female was married in 1998, during the second-follow-up study. She and her husband have settled outside of Minami.

The boys from middle working class families have also gone on to lead middle class lives, though somewhat differently from the girls. Five of the nine were still single in 1998, with three of them still living with their parents in Minami. Seven of them were businessmen, one was a public worker and the other worked in a hotel.

There was one exception to this pattern of middle class life. One young man among them failed college entrance exams and as a result became mentally challenged. When talking with his mother in the summer of 1998, she said that his failure to gain college entrance created psychological disorders for her son. He had lived at home ever since and had not worked in the twelve years since failing the exams.

One distinctive feature of the young adults in this class sub-group was their volunteer work in the community. Two of the middle working class Minami females were leaders of the Girl Scouts and one male was a leader of the Cub Scouts. Perhaps, given their circumstances, the way they kept out of trouble in pursuit of a good education and job, it is not surprising that these young adults appreciated the importance of conventional supportive activities for adolescents. Thus, they have volunteered their time to help provide a meaningful and worthwhile direction for the next generation.

Middle class Hoku youths at higher ranked high schools

Nearly seventy-five percent (17 of 23) of the middle class Hoku youths attended higher ranked high schools. The transition from adolescence to early adulthood for this vast majority of middle class Hoku youths contrasted with that for the Hoku rebels, who were academic underachievers. One-third of them attended private high schools, with slightly more than fifty percent (9 of 17) of these being located outside of Kaigan. Forty-one percent (7 of 17) of their high schools were upper ranked, while fifty-nine percent (10 of 17) of the schools were middle ranked.

Middle class Hoku families have a similar class background to Minami middle working class families. Even so, they are generally wealthier, as indicated by their more expensive and higher quality homes in a more well to do suburb and that fewer mothers in these families worked. All but two middle class Hoku youths that attended higher ranked high schools came from two-parent families. (At the time of the first interviews, the fathers of two of the girls had recently died.) Eleven of their fathers were business-men, two worked in retail shops, one was an architect and one was a public employee. The large majority of mothers were housewives (thirteen in all) and the four working mothers held part- or full-time jobs of a middle class status. Of the nine families about which the parents' educational status is known, eight fathers were college graduates, the other one being a high school graduate, and all nine mothers' were high school graduates.

Hoku middle class girls

All ten middle class Hoku girls at higher ranked high schools were either attending or had just graduated from high school when I first interviewed them. Half of these girls attended private all-girls high schools. With the exception of one girl who fairly actively misbehaved, they all led very conservative, conforming adolescent lives.

The five middle class Hoku females at all-girls private high schools reported a low average of 1.6 acts of misbehavior. Two reported no acts, while two others reported one act of misbehavior each. One did not date during adolescence, two had their first date as high school students and another began dating when she was eighteen. Only two of them had been to a game center.

All-girls high schools are generally stricter than co-ed high schools and although these girls' high schools were strict, the girls themselves did not complain about this aspect of their schooling. This raises an important point about strict high schools. It is the broader social context in which strict school rules and inspections occur that has an effect on student's perceptions and behavior in reaction to these school controls not the rules themselves. Thus, students at low ranked high schools objected to harsh school regulations (enforcement that at times included teacher violence) because they were perceived to be in anticipation of student misbehavior and that, for the students, reinforced the stigma associated with the school's low rank and derogated reputation. At all-girls high schools, however, strict school rules were not maintained in the expectation of student non-conformity, but rather as a way upholding a tradition of order and discipline. Teachers there were not violent. On the contrary, they were very polite and well mannered, with the female teachers especially acting as role models for the students. This did not mean that these girls liked all the rules and regulations, but the strictness of the school existed in a wider context of social conformity and as such did not affect the students' relations with their teachers nor their attachment to the school.

These girls liked their all-girls high schools, though one liked her school at the beginning and then became more ambivalent about it later on. One girl liked school because as, she said, 'it was neat, all of us girls together.' They all got on well with their teachers expressing a liking for teachers such as one saying 'it was a strict school but the teachers were very enthusiastic in their teaching' and another that 'teachers freely gave advice to students.' Three of the students were quite proud of their school, but one did not feel especially proud of her school. One girl, looking back on her high school days, said that the last year in high school was the happiest time of her life.

Five other Hoku girls went to public and private co-ed high schools. Two girls attended the same upper ranked high school in Kaigan and another three went to different middle ranked high schools outside of the city.

Girls at co-ed high schools were less conforming in their behavior compared to girls at all-girls high schools. They averaged two acts of misbehavior, the range being from none to five acts. Just one of these five females dated and went to game centers during high school.

Only one of these youths reported any misbehavior (i.e., drinking alcohol) while at middle school. Misbehavior began in late adolescence and was typical non-conforming behavior for middle class youths. Two of the girls first drank alcohol at ages sixteen and seventeen, two played truant when seventeen, one caused a public disturbance, one went to a drinking establishment at seventeen and two smoked cigarettes at age eighteen.

With the exception of one student that was lukewarm in her feelings about high school, all these Hoku female youths liked their high schools. The schools were not as strict as all-girls high schools and two students said that their school had quite an open and free atmosphere. Again, all but one of the students reported having good relationships with their teachers and of being proud of their school. One youth did good schoolwork, while the academic achievement of another was below average. The other three were average in their school achievements. None of these students got into trouble at school.

Activities of Hoku middle class girls

These middle class Hoku girls were heavily involved in conventional middle class youth activities. They belonged to high school clubs, which included activities such as: tennis, *kendo*, volleyball, badminton, softball, photography and English. Unlike the Hoku rebels and the lower working class Minami adolescents, many of these Hoku females were also involved in middle class activities outside of school. One girl was a leader (den mother) of the Cub Scouts, another had pen pals in Europe, one traveled with her friends to far away places in Japan such as Okinawa, another was an avid skier and yet another was a keen ice skater.

In contrast to lower working class Minami youths, only one of these middle class Hoku high school students worked part-time and two worked as private tutors when in college (a common form of employment for college students in Japan). Freed from the need to work, these middle class high school students could dedicate themselves to the task of preparing for college entrance exams and enjoy taking part in school club activities.

Maiko

Maiko's story is quite typical for a middle class Hoku girl. An only child in a two parent family, she lived at home and attended a middle ranked private all-girls high school outside of Kaigan. Her father, a college graduate, was a businessman, while her mother was a high school graduate and a housewife.

Maiko liked her all-girls high school and appreciated the guidance provided by her teachers. She said the school was strict but thought that was a good thing as it reflected the school's concern that students learn to lead an upright life. Maiko's schoolwork was of an average standard, but she excelled in music and was a particularly good pianist. She later attended a junior college, majoring in childhood education.

Maiko had good relationships with her parents, though she thought they were a little strict about what time she should get home from an outing, etc. Despite this, she thought of her parents more as elder siblings than as adult authority figures. After graduating from junior college she worked for a company, which she had left by the time of the final follow-up study. Then, when I was last in contact with her, she was single and was working part-time in childhood education.

Youth/parent relations among Hoku middle class girls

There was more variation in the girls' responses regarding their home lives than there was about their school lives. Nearly all were conformist at school but their lives at home were less predictable, which shed some light on the culture of modern middle class adolescent females.

Asked if they would feel ashamed if their parents knew they were misbehaving, most of these adolescent girls said that it wasn't shame that inhibited them from getting into trouble. The majority of them believed that misbehavior was bad in and of itself and apart from that feared getting into trouble with adults particularly their parents. The main parental deterrent was the girls' desire not to disappoint their parents; this was consistent with all the other youth sub-class groups.

Parents do not want their children to commit youth crimes, even though the parents themselves often do the very things (e.g., smoking, drinking, etc.) that are defined as acts of misbehavior when done by their children. Despite this seeming hypocrisy, it makes sense that the closer a child feels to her or his parents, the less likely she or he is to want to disobey their demands. However, it was only among Hoku middle class youths that misbehavior correlated at all with the closeness of the youth/parent relationship. In other words, a youth's parental attachment had no bearing on their self-reported rate of misbehavior in any of the other three youth sub-class groups.

Four girls with contrasting self-reported rates of misbehavior differed in parental attachment. Two girls, one of whom had reported a single act of misbehavior, the other who reported none, had closer relations with their parents than two other girls who were comparatively more active in committing youth crimes (they reported three and five acts of misbehavior respectively). While school life also had some influence – the conforming girls attended all-girls high schools while the more rebellious girls attended co-ed schools – there was more variation in the girls' parental attachment than their school attachment.

The two girls who reported only one act of misbehavior between them had extremely good relationships with their parents. One of them wanted to become like her parents, hoping to emulate the 'kindness' of her mother and to be 'trusting' like her father. The other girl related to her parents as if they were her friends. Though she said they worried too much about her, they also trusted her. Both girls said they felt very close to each of their parents.

In contrast, the two more actively misbehaving girls did not care much about their parents. One complained that her parents were too strict, saying that they 'always say don't, don't, don't. So I just don't listen anymore.' Both girls did not get on well with their father and did not wish to be like him. One said that neither a sense of parental shame nor a desire not to disappoint her parents inhibited her misbehavior. She didn't care how they would feel if they knew she misbehaved. The other girl said she didn't feel close to her parents because 'they are old-fashioned – they have that old-fashioned way of thinking and that creates a distance between us.'

The remaining six females, including one who reported the most (i.e., six) acts of misbehavior had parental relationships that were in keeping with those of most youths. As one would expect during adolescence, all six girls felt that their parents only partially understood them. They wanted to be somewhat like their parents but recognizing generation differences, also wished to be different from them. These girls were divided over which parent they felt closest to, though all spent more time with their mother. There was nothing outstandingly negative or positive in their relations with their parents.

A very guarded middle class lifestyle characterized these Hoku girls' transition from adolescence to early adulthood. They all lived in an upper-middle class community, were raised in middle class homes and their education, at least up until college, took place within the conforming context of the middle class student populations of higher ranked high schools.

Hoku middle class boys

Hoku middle class boys that attended higher ranked high schools were more active in committing acts of misbehavior than their female counterparts. This conforms to the conventional notion that boys misbehave more than girls and, again, is reflected in juvenile delinquent statistics that boys have higher official crime rates than do girls. Still, their average rate of three acts of misbehavior is considerably less than that of both their lower working class contemporaries and the male 'Hoku rebels.' The pattern of their misbehavior is very middle class; the 'crimes' committed were not particularly rebellious and they occurred late in their adolescence.

The rate of reported misbehavior for these seven Hoku middle class boys ranged from zero to six acts. The two most common acts of misbehavior were reading pornographic magazines and drinking alcohol while either at middle and/or high school. One such place where Hoku boys read pornographic magazines and drank alcohol was close to their homes. In Hoku there are hideout spots in the surrounding mountains where boys, singly or with their friends, go to read pornographic magazines. They also drink beer there. On many occasions I found scattered beer cans and pornographic magazines purposefully left behind at these hideouts. Pornographic magazines and beer can both be purchased by youths from vending machines, when no adults are looking.

They committed other acts of misbehavior while in high school or during their first year in college. Ranging in age from fifteen to eighteen, three of seven violated the curfews and went to a drinking establishment, two were truant and smoked cigarettes and one had gone to a club or cabaret. These acts of misbehavior all took place outside of Hoku, usually at one of the many entertainment districts in Kanagawa prefecture or in Tokyo. High school and college students have no trouble finding taverns or pubs willing to serve minors and it was not uncommon for Hoku boys to go drinking with their friends during their senior year of high school or after entering college.

These boys had enjoyable experiences of high school. Four of the seven attended upper ranked high schools, while the other three went to middle ranked high schools. Four of them went to high schools in Kaigan, one to a private, all-boys upper ranked high school, the others to co-ed schools. All liked high school saying, for example, they had fun at school or they liked high school because of their friendships there. All got along well with their teachers, though some teachers were liked more than others. A few students particularly stressed that they had very good relations with teachers.

The boys achieved good academic results, with three of them receiving above average grades. They were all proud of their schools. One was proud because, he said, his high school is 'quite famous so I feel good if someone asks me the name of the school I go to.' And another said, 'I went there since middle school [his middle school was connected to the high school]. This strengthened my love for the school and allowed me to naturally be myself. I liked the school atmosphere; we could freely speak our mind.'

Activities of Hoku middle class boys

Similar to Hoku middle class girls at higher ranked high schools, these middle class boys were heavily involved in conventional middle class youth activities. Most belonged to a high school club, covering such activities as tennis, volleyball, track and archery. One boy trained in *kendo* at a private *kendo* club. None of these youths worked part-time while still at secondary school. Rather they were kept busy with club activities and in preparing for college entrance examinations.

Atsushi

Atsushi's family background, school life and transition into early adulthood can be considered as reasonably representative of other middle class Hoku boys that attended higher ranked high schools. He was born and raised in Hoku and had just entered one of the better Japanese universities when we first met. He lived with both his parents and a younger brother and his grandfather lived next door to them. His father, a college graduate, was a businessman, while his mother, a high school graduate, was a housewife.

Atsushi had attended the co-joining all-boys upper ranked middle and high school located in Kaigan. His schoolwork was of a high standard. Quite a few Hoku boys went to this school, which was popular among the youths. He described the school as relaxed, said he had close relationships with his teachers and was quite proud of his school. He also was a member of the school's Tennis Club.

Atsushi, like many Hoku boys, had a positive outlook on life. His colleagues at the school were from similar higher-class backgrounds, most lived in Kaigan and were involved in club activities. During our interview, Atsushi made an interesting comment about Shonan. Shonan had the reputation among Kaigan youths as a rough place. Atsushi had never been to Shonan but said that Shonan high school students were thought to be *kowai* (scary or dangerous).

Despite his attachment to his school, his involvement in conventional youth activities and his good relations with his parents, Atsushi was no angel. One must be careful not to equate conformity with blandness or sameness, for each adolescent has her/his own way. At fourteen Atsushi first drank alcohol, at fifteen he dated and went to game centers, at sixteen he read pornographic magazines and when seventeen he smoked cigarettes. While such a pattern of misbehavior was not nearly as defiant as those of the lower working class Minami youths or the Hoku rebels, it was still significant and suggests that a certain amount of deviant youth behavior is merely a part of growing up.

After graduating from college Atsushi became a businessman like his father. At the time of the final follow-up study he was married with one child. His wife, like his mother, was a housewife.

Youth/parent relations among middle class Hoku boys

One of the Hoku middle class boys differed substantially from his peers in his attachment to his parents. While Yasuhiro was reasonably attached to his high school, he was relatively unattached to his parents. He did not have a close relationship with either parent and he said that his parents didn't understand him and that he did not want to be like them at all. Of the seven middle class boys, Yasuhiro reported the highest number of acts of misbehavior (i.e., six). Yasuhiro also stated that he would feel no shame if his parents knew that he misbehaved. Also, he was one of the few youths in the whole study that said a desire not to want to disappoint his parents in no way inhibited his misbehavior. He didn't care about his parent's feelings rather he thought it simple common sense to stay out of trouble.

The other six middle class boys all felt at least quite close to their parents. Most of them stated that their parents understood some things about them and not others. They generally wanted to become like their parents, at least to some degree. Some of them were closer to one parent or the other, but there was no mention of any of them disliking either parent.

Adolescent life for these middle class Hoku boys was very similar to that of the girls, except the boys misbehaved more frequently. They went to good schools that had conformist student populations and experienced no trouble with adult authority at school or in the area where they lived. Their acts of misbehavior began at an older age and were less serious than those of the lower working class Minami youths and the Hoku rebels.

One reason middle class Hoku boys misbehaved more than the girls of their class was their gender-specific socialization. Half of the girls were separated from the boys during adolescence and were sent to extremely conservative, middle class higher ranked girls' high schools. Even at the higher ranked co-ed secondary schools, gender interaction was limited, with boys and girls spending most of their spare time in same-sex sporting clubs. Dating was not the norm until late-adolescence. Such girls were schooled in female middle class etiquette and were expected to abide by adult standards for youth behavior. Deviation from adult expectations of female middle class behavior was truly an exception among middle class Hoku girls and this pattern of conformity was continued into their early adulthood.

Hoku middle class young adults

Only one female did not go on to further education after high school graduation. After finishing high school, she worked full-time for a private railway company, then married a businessman and in 1999 was a housewife with two children in elementary school. One of the young women studied interior design at a special school and married a fellow special school graduate. When we last met near her parent's home in 1999, they had no children, her husband was unemployed and she was working part-time as an interior designer. Three of the six Hoku middle class females graduated from junior colleges. Young women generally attend junior (2 year) colleges rather than four-year colleges. Many junior colleges are all-girls schools and are widely considered to be 'breeding' grounds for marriage. Over ninety percent of junior college students are female (Andressen and Gainey 2002: 164). Female students in these colleges are primed in female etiquette and most have a major in foreign languages, the humanities, home economics or the arts. At the time of the final follow-up study, two of the three junior college graduates were married. One was a housewife with a child in elementary school and her husband was a businessman. Another had married a businessman, was childless and worked part-time. The only single female junior college graduate was living in her parent's home and was working part-time at a kindergarten. Two of the three female four-year college graduates were married and each had two children. One was a housewife, married to a businessman. The other worked as a pharmacist and though her husband was employed she didn't disclose the nature of his job. The single female four-year college graduate worked for a company in Tokyo.

All the middle class Hoku boys went straight from higher ranked high schools into college and are now all college graduates. Five of the seven graduated from a four-year college and two are junior college graduates. Five of them are married, with all but one of these having children. In 1999 they were all enjoying a middle class lifestyle, with six of them working as businessmen for Japanese companies and the one working from home, having set-up his own small business. One of the seven works for his grandfather's company in Tokyo and already holds a managerial position, while the others are all on track towards managerial positions in the companies for which they work.

Middle class Hoku youths that attended higher ranked high schools had, from birth onwards, grown-up in very conformist surroundings. They have all been the recipients of a very conforming middle class lifestyle, one that has been reproduced in the lives they are now leading as young adults.

Upper class Hoku youths

The social status family backgrounds of the twenty-six upper class Hoku youths that I interviewed are quite impressive. Twelve of them had fathers who were businessmen that, all indicators (educational background, nice Hoku home, wife's working status and in some cases company background information) suggest, occupied at least lower managerial positions at large, well-known Japanese companies. Eight of their fathers occupied high-status positions, including a president of a company, the manager of an industrial plant, a landowner, two college professors, an architect and the father of two sisters was a well-known artist. Two fathers were government employees, three were secondary school teachers and one was an elementary school teacher. All but two of their mothers were housewives and the two that were employed were professionals, one a high school teacher, the other a piano teacher. All but one of the fathers (the wealthy landowner) graduated from college and all but one of the mothers (the wife of the wealthy landowner) were either college graduates (74%) or special school graduates (26%).

Given these class privileges, upper class Hoku youths went to the best schools. Fifteen of twenty-six students attended upper ranked high schools, most (12) of them at upper ranked high schools in Kaigan. The other ten students went to middle ranked high schools. (The high school rank of one of the youths is not known.) Their families' high incomes enabled them to be properly prepared (e.g., tutors, cram schools, etc.) for gaining entrance into these schools. Furthermore, their well-educated mothers were at home to supervise their study or, in the case of the two working mothers, they were both teachers and were therefore well equipped to assist their children. These youths had all these advantages from birth and as such led the most privileged adolescent lives of all the youths in this study.

Nineteen Hoku girls and seven Hoku boys came from upper class families. The higher proportion of females in Hoku's adolescent population (70% were females) is reflected in this gender imbalance.

Upper class Hoku girls

Upper class Hoku females had a low average of 2.2 acts of misbehavior. Their pattern of misbehavior was also quite conservative taking place at an older adolescent age and involving less serious acts of youth misconduct. Their two most common types of misbehavior – reported by more than half of them – were drinking alcohol and going to a drinking establishment. Most, however, reported that they first did these things when they were eighteen years old. Fifteen was the youngest age reported for drinking and seventeen for going to a drinking establishment. At eighteen, all but one of these females (a special school student) were college students and it is more or less accepted that drinking and going to drinking establishments is a part of the initiation rite for first year college students.

A small minority of upper class Hoku females reported other acts of misbehavior. Between the ages of sixteen and eighteen, five of them had been truants and four had broken the curfew. Two of them reported having smoked when aged sixteen and seventeen respectively, and two had played *pachinko* at seventeen. Single reported acts of misbehavior included going to a bar aged eighteen and reading a pornographic magazine at fifteen.

Complimentary with that very few upper class Hoku females engaged in non-normative youth misconduct (drinking and frequenting a drinking establishment when in college is normative behavior), they also led very protected adolescent lives. Six of them never dated during adolescence and most had had their first date at age seventeen or eighteen. A little less than half had never been to a game center and all but two had experienced absolutely no trouble at school; two of them were scolded at school, one for having a hair permanent, the other for leaving school early one day.

Seven girls attended private all-girls high schools. Three of the four high schools that they attended had adjoining middle schools and the one that didn't adjoined an affiliated college. Six of the girls had gone to an adjoining middle school and one went to the affiliated college after graduating from its high school. Four of the girls attended two schools that were well known as elite, upper ranked all-girls schools. The other three students went to various middle ranked all-girls schools. Although these all-girls high schools were strict, all but two girls were strongly attached to their school.

Typically, the girls said that their teachers were excellent instructors and all but one claimed to have very good relationships with their teachers. All of these upper class Hoku female students were reasonably high academic achievers, with five receiving above average grades and another two doing average schoolwork. All were proud of their school.

One girl though, Yuka, differed from her upper class Hoku peers, because over time she rebelled against the strict rules at her all-girls high school. As a first year student, she had liked her high school and got on reasonably well with her teachers. After graduation, though, looking back at her high school life, Yuka complained that the school was too strict and told the story of how, after first year, she got into trouble for violating school hairstyle regulations regarding perms. Having also attended the adjoining middle school, Yuka said that six years in the one institution was too long a time and that she felt ambivalent about the school. After first year, she occasionally played truant and her academic standards dropped from above average to average.

Eight of the twelve females that attended higher ranked co-ed high schools went to two different upper ranked schools in Kaigan. Both schools were said by these students to be liberal in regards to regulations and made comments such as, 'students have freedom' or 'we were free' in expressing their liking for the school. All were at least moderately proud of their school, many suggesting with pride that they attended a 'good school' or a school with a good atmosphere. For all but one of these students, teacher relations were especially good and were characterized by trust and understanding. These students did well in their studies, with three receiving above average grades, three average grades and only one of them receiving below average grades.

A main feature of upper ranked high schools in Kaigan is the higher-class homogeneity of the students who attend them. Most of the students of these schools lived in Kaigan, a city considered to be higher-class in Japan. This reinforced conformity and enhanced school solidarity. Students said they liked school because of the friendships they had there, and some even mentioned feeling close to other students because of their like-mindedness.

Kana, though, was an exception to this rule. She attended an upper-ranked high school in Kaigan, really liked the teachers and was very proud of school, but didn't like the 'sameness' of students. In the first follow-up study, she stated that she felt 'so-so' about her high school. Kana explained why, 'In high school, students were all the same but in middle school there were different kinds of students and the way of thinking was more diverse, so I had more fun with my school friends in middle school.'

The remaining four upper class Hoku girls attended different middle ranked co-ed high schools, all but one located outside of Kaigan. They were less attached to and not as proud of their high schools as upper class females at upper ranked high schools. Still, they all got on fairly well with their teachers and none of them disliked their school. Their slightly weaker attachment to school had no bearing on their misbehavior, which were no different from those of students at upper ranked high schools. Simply, these four students were not high academic achievers in middle school and therefore could not get into upper ranked high schools. Their academic achievement in high school also was lower than Hoku girls at upper ranked high schools: one student received excellent grades, two average grades and one below average grades.

Activities of upper class Hoku girls

Upper class Hoku girls were very actively involved in conventional middle class youth activities. Almost every one of them was a member of a high school club, that included activities such as, aikido and judo, basketball, dance, *kendo*, tennis, table tennis, athletics, handball and English. Of all the girls interviewed, they were also the most active in extracurricular youth activities. Two girls took private piano lessons for a number of years and two others practiced the arts of painting and photography. One girl had, for many years, been a member of a private *kendo* school, another belonged to a private tennis club, one girl studied English at a private English conversation school and one was a leader of the YMCA. Only one upper class Hoku girl worked part-time while still at high school. Some college students did conventional part-time work as private tutors, preparing younger students for high school and college entrance examinations.

Emi

Emi's adolescence and early adulthood was reasonably representative of the upper class Hoku adolescent girls that attended upper ranked high schools in Kaigan. Born in Hoku, she lived in a beautiful, expansive home with a meticulous garden located on top of a mountain. She shared this house with her parents, grandmother, an elder sister and a younger brother. Emi was cognizant of her higher-class status, acknowledging that the family was upper middle class. Her father, a college graduate, was a successful businessman, while her mother, a special school graduate, was a housewife.

The upper ranked high school that she attended was well liked among Hoku youth. Emi, like many of her fellow students, mentioned the school's liberal approach to rules and regulations and that it had a free, open and very relaxed atmosphere. She was also proud of the school. Emi said that one reason the school was not strict was because the students caused absolutely no problems. She liked the teachers because she felt they were always there for the students and that she could talk with them about anything, not just school-related matters.

Emi was a member of her high school Handball Club and was a good student. She, along with her three best friends, kept out of trouble, though, like her, two of her friends dated. Emi had been dating since she was fourteen, which is quite young for an upper class Hoku girl. Emi had excellent relationships with her parents throughout her time in high school and college. When she was in high school her parents were reasonably strict about her studies, emphasizing their desire for her to attend a good university. Still, they trusted her and every Sunday the whole family went out to dinner together. Even as a college student, she still felt very close to them. She often went out shopping with her father and felt free to say anything she wanted to her parents and even talked to them about her boyfriend.

Emi graduated from one of the better universities in Japan and later married a college graduate. By 1999 they had a small child. Emi was a housewife and her husband was working in real estate.

Youth/parent relations among upper class Hoku girls

Quite a few upper class girls complained about their parents, particularly their mothers, being too strict. The issue was typically about the need for them to study hard in preparation for high school and college entrance exams. The consequences of this friction varied. For example, Yayoi complained that her parents were too strict. She quarreled with them about the need for her to study so hard for college entrance exams. Even after entering college, though, her parents still got upset if she came home late, asking her where she had been, why she was late, and so on. They were over protective and were always warning her about the dangers of this and that. Despite not liking her parents' over-protectiveness, Yayoi still felt very close to them. She knew they cared about her and sought their advice, rather than that of friends or teachers, concerning important matters.

When taken to extremes, parental strictness could have negative consequences. Having gone through all the right preparations (cram schools since middle school etc.) in order to gain entry into an upper ranked high school in Kaigan, Mayumi was now preparing for college entrance exams. Her father, a Tokyo University graduate, was very strict about her study. College entrance exams are held in February, but she was more or less forced to stay at home to study for these exams from the previous summer onwards. The only time Mayumi was allowed out during that summer was to go to see a volleyball match. This, though, resulted in her father's rage when she came home just a little late.

Unyielding parental pressure made Mayumi feel guilty when she was not studying. She always kept her books with her and became neurotic about studying. Outside of the home, she kept her eyes focused on the ground fearing eye contact. Mayumi's neurosis reached the point that she thought that if her eyes met with someone else's they would instantly recognize that she should be studying and would then become upset with her. This kept her at home and even when she had no more energy to study, she kept her books close by to remind her that she should be studying.

Another feature of youth/parent relations for upper class Hoku girls was generation value differences, which usually resulted in them having conflict with their mothers. One girl complained that her mother was too rigid and stated that she didn't want to become like that. Another girl felt her mother was a real perfectionist, she was neurotic about everything being just right, and she too did not want to be like her mother. One girl said that her father did not understand her because he was old fashioned in his ideas about the difference between females and males. Two other girls rebelled against the idea of becoming housewives like their mothers.

These upper class Hoku girls lived in homes where, although their mothers were well educated, they were stuck being housewives. Having been encouraged to succeed academically, and having attended the very best schools, it seemed anachronistic to these girls that, regardless of their education or personal aspirations, if they married they were destined to become housewives. This questioning of the traditional gender roles created generation tensions. Mami, for example, did not have a close relationship with her mother and had decided that if in the future she were to marry she did not want to be a housewife like her mother. Instead, she wanted to have her own career.

Mami also didn't get along with her father. Though she wouldn't say exactly what caused their rift, something happened in her third year of middle school that made her strongly dislike him. At the time of our first interview, they hadn't talked for more than two years. Her dislike of both parents and her conviction not to become like her mother both found expression in the life she chose as an adult. Having studied at the prestigious Tokyo University of Agriculture, Mami later married her college sweetheart, moved far away from home to the northern part of Japan and, like her husband and despite having a small child, she now works full-time for the national government.

Another girl, Minako, also did not want to follow her mother's path and become a housewife. She respected her father because he was skillful at whatever he did and decided to become a career woman. After high school graduation, Minako went to a special school where she majored in broadcasting. During our last talk together in 1999, she mentioned that her lover of eight years proposed marriage a number of times but she likes her job and her life as it is and has turned him down each time. Minako works in broadcasting for a major Japanese television station.

Kumiko was the only girl who had a weak attachment to both her higher ranked high school and her parents. She was also the most misbehaved upper class Hoku female, reporting five youth offences. At the time of our first interview and again three years later, after she had graduated from college during the first follow-up study, Kumiko voiced a dislike for her upper ranked high school. The classes, she said, weren't interesting and her relation with teachers was at best average. Kumiko also didn't get on well with her parents. Communication at home was poor and she felt her parents didn't understand her at all. 'I don't tell my parents much about my life' she said. 'We don't really talk much about anything.'

Overall, though, there was more conflict at home than at school for upper class Hoku females. This, however, had no bearing on their misbehavior, as they all reported very few acts of misbehavior regardless of whether they got along with their parents or not. Besides the cases just cited, the majority of the upper class Hoku girls got along fairly well with their parents. Some had better relations with one parent than with the other, but nothing about their parental relations differentiated them from all the other youths in the study. What clearly was an advantage for these girls was that more than any other sub-class group their parents provided them with the opportunity to go to the best schools and this both afforded them a good education and also kept them out of trouble. Today these upper class youths are quite successful young adults; much like their parents' expected them to be.

Upper class Hoku boys

Upper class Hoku boys misbehaved more than their female peers, averaging a little over three acts of misbehavior, though this was skewed by two boys having reported five and nine acts of misbehavior respectively. The misbehavior of these upper class boys was, however, not part of an anti-school subculture, as they all attended higher ranked high schools. The patterns of their misbehavior showed variability in the level of conformity among upper class boys, yet, because of the area in which they lived and their families' social class privileges occasional acts of misbehavior did not have a negative impact on their future adult lives.

The one who reported the highest number of acts of misbehavior, Yuichi, exhibited a pattern of misbehavior similar to lower working class Minami youths. While still at middle school he smoked cigarettes, violated the curfew, played truant, read a pornographic magazine and dated. Then, in high school, he drank alcohol, frequented drinking establishments and other places off-limits to youths, was sexually active and hung-out at game centers.

Yuichi did not care much for his high school, saying that having to spend all that time in a classroom everyday was no fun. He was often absent from school and had fun with his friends and the school authorities caught him both smoking and being truant. He was given a warning, yet still managed to make it through high school and on to college. Again, at college, Yuichi was mischievous and was caught drinking and setting off fireworks by the police. Interestingly, nothing much was made of these 'crimes' and he was not officially sanctioned for his misconduct.

Yasuhiro too was fairly active in committing youth offences, though he was not as rebellious as lower working class Minami youths or the male Hoku rebels. While still at middle school, he went to a game center and violated the curfew. But it was while in high school that he really began to have his fun. At sixteen he reported smoking, drinking, reading pornography and having gone to a drinking establishment. Still, Yasuhiro really liked his high school, had good relationships with his teachers, never got into any trouble at school and was reasonably proud of the school. He, like Yuichi, went on to college.

Area and family social class advantages clearly made for a different transition into young adulthood for Yuichi and Yasuhiro compared with that made by lower working class Minami youths with similar patterns of misbehavior. Both boys went to higher ranked high schools. Yuichi's grades were above average and he said that his high school was not at all strict. Yasuhiro's grades were average, but he was quite attached to his high school. Both boys were also involved in conventional youth activities. Beyond this, their class privileges and that they lived in Hoku rather than Minami meant that nothing was made of their misbehavior.

The other five upper class Hoku boys hardly misbehaved at all, with the range of their self-reported acts being from zero to three. Two of the five attended a co-joining upper ranked all-boys middle/high school. One went to a middle ranked high school and another went to a co-ed upper ranked high school in Kaigan. (One was a middle school student that moved out of Hoku and could not be found during the follow-up studies. Thus, information about his secondary schooling is unknown.) All these boys received above average or average grades in their studies. All mentioned having a good school life and were closely attached to their schools and teachers.

Activities of upper class Hoku boys

Six of the seven boys were involved in conventional middle class youth clubs. During middle school, one was a captain of his school's tennis team, another belonged to an athletic club, one was a Boy Scout and another belonged to the school's Science Club. In high school, one boy belonged to the Soccer Club and another to the school's History Club. None of the boys worked part-time during their secondary schooling.

Akio

Akio's story characterizes the elite way of life enjoyed by male upper class Hoku youths. Born in Hoku, he went to the same popular upper ranked high school in Kaigan as Emi. He was a third year student at the time of our first of many encounters. Akio lived in a large and attractive house on top of a mountain, from which he could enjoy a great view of Hoku. His father graduated from a very prestigious fine arts university and worked as an illustrator in a large company. His mother was a housewife.

Akio was an idealist. At one time he wanted to be an English teacher but then changed his mind and hoped some day to work for an international agency that dealt with education in third world countries. To realize this dream, he quit the school's Soccer Club in his final year of high school and studied hard in order to win a place at one of the best universities in Japan.

Akio thought very highly of his father. His father was a hard worker but was still readily available when his son needed advice or to just talk with him on the weekends. Akio also liked his mother but felt she was a little selfish. He really enjoyed living in such a nice place like Hoku.

Although Akio and his friends experimented with smoking and drinking, it was just that – experimentation. When in their last year of high school, they were all preparing for college entrance exams and no longer saw much of each other.

As it was, Akio failed to pass the college entrance exam for one of the top three universities and was planning to try again the following year. He asked me to help him with his English. I agreed, but he never followed through with it. Some time later his whole family moved to California and, as a result, I never found out what became of him.

Youth/parent relations among upper class Hoku boys

Yuichi, the upper class boy who misbehaved the most, also had the most distant relations with his parents. He did not want to become like his mother or his father. In fact, he said that he didn't want to be like anyone else – that he was his own person. The other six upper class boys got on fairly well with their parents, with none of them mentioning any troubles at home.

Upper class Hoku youths as young adults

Upper-class Hoku youths had a smooth transition into early adulthood and now lead middle class lifestyles that are on the road towards being upper class. Only one of them was a high school graduate, two graduated from a special school and eighteen were college graduates. And, for the females, unlike their middle class Hoku contemporaries, half of whom were junior college graduates, eleven of fifteen upper class females graduated from four-year colleges; the remaining four being junior college graduates. Interestingly, these young women were also the most career-minded of all the sub-class grouping of females.

In 1999, all of the six single, upper class Hoku females were working, three of them in professional careers. Three of them worked as office ladies in small companies, one taught flower arranging (*ikebana* in Japanese a traditional art), one was a stewardess for JAL (Japan Airlines – the most prestigious airline in Japan) and another worked in broadcasting for a major Japanese television station. Among the twelve married females, two with children had professional careers; one had married an Englishman and was living with him and their child in England (her working status is unknown) and another who had a small child worked, along with her husband, for the national government. Still another, who had three children, continued to work as a nurse.

Among the males, since the original study, one had moved with his family to America and three others had moved with their families to unknown locations. Three of the upper class males responded to both follow-up studies. One of these had attended an elite, all-boys upper-ranked high school, had graduated from college and then went on to graduate school and obtained a Master of Arts in the Sociology of Law. He then later studied chiropractic medicine. At our last contact, he was a licensed chiropractor, was single and still living at home in Hoku with his parents. Yasuhiro, who had graduated from a four-year college, was single and was living in Tokyo, where he was working as a businessman. Yuichi went on to graduate from a four-year college, was married and was working as a businessman. His wife was a housewife.

In 1999 four of the eight single young adults and three of the married females, two of them whom had children, were still living at home. While my information regarding their married lives was incomplete, marrying one's college sweetheart or meeting one's future spouse at work was the most common means of mate-selection. Given that companies recruit people from similar family and educational backgrounds (even targeting specific colleges), *shokuba kekkon* (marriage at the workplace) entails marrying someone from the same family social class background. The husbands of most Hoku females were business-men and the wife of the only Hoku male who by that time had married was a housewife.

The upper class Hoku adults' responses to questions regarding husband-wife relations indicated that none of them had any serious marital problems and none were divorced. Class endogamy (marrying within the same class) was the norm, thus facilitating the social reproduction of class and increasing the chances of family support for the marriage.

These twenty-six upper class Hoku youths led privileged lives throughout their adolescence. Although they appeared to be conformists, attending good schools, some at the best in the prefecture, conflict was not absent from their lives. A few temporarily flaunted middle class values and engaged in acts of misbehavior. They did this for fun, knowing they wouldn't face any serious consequences from their misconduct. For the females, family conflict derived from generation differences regarding the roles of women and mothers. These girls had been educated in the best schools and it didn't make sense to them that, like their mothers, they too should have to limit their lives to the role of being a housewife. Now, in their late twenties or early thirties, these upper class Hoku young adults, both male and female, are pursuing careers that potentially lead to high status occupations.

Educational attainment

Table 5.1 presents the completed education level of Minami and Hoku youths broken down by parental social class and level of conformity. Educational attainment is almost exactly the same among conformists and non-conformists. Less than fourteen percent of rebellious youths (Minami lower working class and Hoku rebels) have a college education. Conformists have a high level of completed education, with eighty-six percent being college graduates. Adding together the Hoku rebels and the Hoku high achievers, two-thirds of middle class Hoku youths attained a college degree. What is remarkable, though, is that Minami middle working class youths have exactly the same, extremely high, college-completion rate as that of Hoku upper class youths and that this rate is seventy-four percent higher than that for Minami lower working class youth.

The figures at the bottom of this table clearly indicate the importance of class ecology and high school rank to educational attainment. Nearly all of the rebellious youths attended low ranked high schools compared to just one conformist who attended such a school. Added to this, not one rebellious youth went to an upper ranked high school. While a good percentage of middle class youths attended upper ranked high schools, it was only among upper class Hoku youths that the majority of students attended

Table 5.1   Behavior during adolescence, social class and educational attainment for Minami and Hoku youth

	Behavior During Adolescence				
	Rebellion		Conformity		
	Social Class		Social Class		
Educational Attainment	Minami Lower Working	Hoku Middle Class Rebels	Minami Middle Working	Hoku Middle Class Achievers	Hoku Upper Class
Middle School % (n)	12.5% (2)	16.6% (1)	0% (0)	0% (0)	0% (0)
High School % (n)	69% (11)	50% (3)	7% (1)	7% (1)	5% (1)
Special School % (n)	6% (1)	16.6% (1)	7% (1)	7% (1)	9% (2)
College % (n)	12.5% (2)	16.6% (1)	86% (12)	86% (13)	86% (18)
Total % (n)	100% (16)	99.8% (6)	100% (14)	100% (15)	100% (21)
% at low ranked high school	82%	100%	7%	0%	0%
% at upper ranked high school	0%	0%	36%	40%	67%
% Minami youth	53%		47%		
% Hoku youth		14%		36%	50%

such schools. Finally, class ecology clearly influenced student conformity and hence educational attainment. Looking at the very last entry in the table, fifty-three percent of Minami youths (all lower working class) are represented in the rebellion category, while eighty-four percent of Hoku youths (all middle and upper class) appear in the conformity category.

Both Table 5.2 ('Minami youth and parents' educational attainment by class') and Table 5.3 ('Hoku youth and parents' educational attainment by class') show how class is socially reproduced through education. In Table 5.2, the low twelve and a half percent of college graduates among lower working class Minami youths almost exactly mirrors the eleven percent of their parent(s) who attained this level of education. The same is true at the other end of the scale. In Table 5.3, the very high eighty-three percent of upper class Hoku parents with a college education is reproduced by the eighty-six percent of upper class Hoku youths that graduated from college.

The economic growth of Japan equates with a higher level of completed education for the younger generation (Rohlen 1983; Sugimoto 2003). This trend was reflected in that the percentage of college education attainment for middle class youth from both Minami and Hoku was higher than that of their parents. Table 5.2 shows that a fairly high sixty percent of Minami working middle class parents are college graduates, but that an even higher eighty-six percent of Minami middle working class youths graduated from college – an increase of twenty-six percent. A similar trend occurred in Hoku, as can be seen in Table 5.3, where forty-one percent of middle class Hoku parents graduated from college and an even higher sixty-seven percent of Hoku middle class youths are college graduates – again, an increase of twenty-six percent.

The only generation variation in educational attainment for lower working class youth that equates with the overall increase of educational qualifications occurred at the level below high school graduation. Nearly half (44%) of Minami lower working class parents failed to graduate from high school, compared to only twelve and a half percent of their adolescent children. Still, the vast majority of both Minami lower working class parents and youths had only a high school education or below and more lower working class families live in Minami than middle working class families.

Table 5.2 Minami youth and parents educational attainment by class

Educational Attainment %	Class			
	Lower-Working Household		Middle-Working Household	
	Youth	Parents	Youth	Parents
Below High School	12.50%	44%	0%	0%
High School	69%	33%	7%	25%
Special School	6%	11%	7%	5%
Some College	0%	0%	0%	10%
College	12.50%	11%	86%	60%
Total %	**100%**	**99%**	**100%**	**100%**

Note: Information on the educational attainment of parent(s) is less complete than youth because it was only gathered during the follow-up studies. Educational attainment of lower-working class parents(s) is more incomplete than any other sub-class group since fewer Minami lower working class youths responded to the follow-up study questionnaires. Given that occupational stratification and working status of mothers were measures of class in the original study, it is doubtful that had information been available educational attainment would differ substantially from that presented here. Among Minami lower working class parent(s) only two had a higher level of education (one had graduated from a special school, the other from college). Despite this they were considered lower working class because of their overall class situation. Both of these adults were single parents of two children, their ex-spouses had a low level of education (less than high school and a high school graduate) and they had very low occupational statuses, one as a cook, the other a gambling operator.

As we have seen, non-conformity or rebellion is closely tied in with class culture and social class: youth-adult conflict arises from the adult social control establishment's preoccupation with preserving the 'status quo.' Demonstrated conformity at an early age, together with the social control establishment's channeling of potential troublemakers (mostly from the lower class) into low ranked high schools created a highly homogenous conforming setting for students (predominantly from the higher classes) at higher ranked high schools. These students then went on to college, obtained the most prestigious jobs and married within their own class, thereby ensuring a continuation of the status quo through the social reproduction of class.

This then leads us to ask why some social conditions are more conducive to deviant youth behavior than others and how such behavior impacts on the lives of youths as they enter early adulthood. The answers to these questions comprise the subject

Table 5.3   Hoku youth and parents educational attainment by class

Educational Attainment %	Class			
	Middle Household		Upper Household	
	Youth	Parents	Youth	Parents
Below High School	5%	0%	0%	0%
High School	19%	54%	5%	2%
Special School	10%	5%	9%	12%
Some College	0%	0%	0%	2%
College	67%	41%	86%	83%

Note: Like Table 5.2, the educational attainment of parents is less complete than that of youth because it was only gathered during the follow-up studies. Given occupational stratification and working status of mothers that were measures of class in the original study and high response rate of both middle and upper class Hoku youths to the follow-up studies, it is doubtful that had all responded to the follow-up studies educational attainment would differ substantially from that presented here.

of the next chapter. In that chapter labeling conflict theory is used to explain the process by which youths engage in deviant behavior, adopt a deviant identity and how this relates to adolescents confronted with a limited set of choices and opportunities for establishing their position in the adult social class hierarchy.

6 Labeling and the Transition into Early Adulthood

Labeling conflict theory

In previous chapters, I have employed theory sparingly and in a piecemeal manner. Various theoretical tenets have been applied to make sense of the situations and conditions of class, area of residence, school life, activities, parental relations and peer group influence on youth crime and the transition from adolescence to early adulthood. This chapter adopts a more holistic theoretical approach to describe and explain the relationship of class ecology to youth crime and the consequences of this on the transition into early adulthood. By integrating and synthesizing information from previous chapters, I will here present a labeling conflict perspective of youth deviance and the transition from adolescence to early adulthood.

Steinhoff's (1984) application of a labeling theory of conflict to the student movement in Japan acts as a template for our discussion here of the process of adolescent transition into early adulthood. Both phenomena entail change involving deviance and conflict. Steinhoff states:

> [A] labeling theory explanation of conflict involves two converging processes: creating and imposing the label of "deviant" on certain acts and persons and the individuals' acceptance of the label as a central feature of their identity' (1984: 195).

The process of transition from adolescence to young adulthood is full of possibilities for escalating deviant behavior and the inculcation of deviant identity. The potential for both of these occurring in a given individual is not however equal, because a youth's class and the area in which they live largely determines the 'availability' of opportunities to misbehave, the amount of adult social control and the extent of the consequences of their deviant behavior. The family class background of youths and others reactions to it also influences the amount of exposure that an adolescent has to imagery and interactions conducive to them taking on a deviant identity.

In describing people, settings and objects involved in the labeling process I will at times utilize Lofland's (1969) concepts of Actor, Others, Places and Hardware. (These concepts will be capitalized when specific reference is made to them.) An Actor is the focus of attention in the labeling process, in this instance, Minami and Hoku youth. Others are people who influence an Actor's behavior and identity. These range from imputation specialists (adult social control agents, such as teachers) to peer group members. Places are the locations where an Actor spends most of his or her time and the reputations given to such locations. Schools and 'youth hangouts' are the Places of central concern here. According to Lofland, Hardware 'is intended to denote both those physical objects that can be attached or affixed to the body of an Actor and those that can be picked up or manipulated' (1969: 174). In this context, school uniform, school paraphernalia and teacher attire are all Hardware items. Others, Places and Hardware interact in ways that create the potential for a given Actor to engage in deviant acts, as well as project a certain image on the perpetuator (Actor) of such acts.

The application of labeling conflict theory to the process of adolescent transition into early adulthood raises a number of key questions. What behavioral alternatives are there for youths growing up in a delinquency-prone area like Minami? What choices could Minami youths make that would lessen their chances of deviant behavior? Why do certain social circumstances and not others encourage deviant behavior and the adoption of a 'deviant identity'? How is it that delinquency control measures discourage rather than assist non-conforming young people to change their behavior, to become more conforming? Why is the social reproduction of class so dominant in determining an adolescent's path into adulthood? And, finally, what social barriers restrict social mobility?

Entry into adolescence and deviant behavior

Except for a few Hoku youths that attended private elementary schools, most youths went to local elementary schools and none made mention of being in trouble in elementary school. The start of middle school attendance marks a child's entrance into adolescence and it is there that differences in deviant behavior and the taking on of a deviant identity began. Hoku students were not exposed to an anti-school subculture, simply because such groups were not present in either the local or private middle schools that they attended. In contrast, all Minami middle school students were confronted with the situation of active student misbehavior and student-school conflict. Thus, young Minami adolescents were introduced to situations conducive to delinquent behavior while their Hoku peers remained protected from them.

The decision of students to join in with the anti-school groups at their middle school had as much to do with their families' social class disadvantages as with the absence of alternative modes of behavior. Delinquency prevention in and around Minami was coercive and punitive. As such, there were no community delinquency prevention volunteers to help disadvantaged students with their homework, nor any initiative to subsidize the costs of a *juku* or tutor for such students.

Delinquency prevention in Japan – ranging from P.T.A. to *hogoshi* (volunteer probation officers) – consists of adult organizations set-up for the purpose of controlling and punishing youth behavior. Delinquency prevention activities publicize the need to steer youths in the right direction, to clean-up areas where delinquency is known to occur and to try to catch youths committing deviant acts and closely monitor them once they have been officially caught in the 'wrong' (Ames 1981; Yoder 1986: 12–19). Hence, these organizations are not concerned with the conditions (minority or class disadvantages) that lead to the onset of delinquency.

Among modern economically developed societies, Japan ranks low in expenditure on social security programs and is not known for a tradition of domestic voluntary and/or charity work (Verba et al. 1987: 10–11; Woronoff 1981). While anti-discriminatory legislation and government assistance for minority groups, particularly the indigenous Burakumin and Ainu groups, has improved over the years, social-economic barriers remain for minorities and the lower class. Ethnic minorities (including Koreans, Chinese, Filipinos, Thai's, South Americans, Middle Easterners, Ainu and Okinawans), visible Japanese minorities (so-called '*hafu*", which translates as half-breed or mixed race children), former outcastes (Burakumin) and lower class families face numerous obstacles when they attempt to join in with the mainstream way of life. Furthermore, unlike in some other countries, there is a noticeable absence of religious organizations offering to help poor families and wayward youths.

Less than one percent of the Japanese population is Christian and the vast majority of Japanese profess to be non-religious. Despite this, *Nihonkyō*, a combination of Shinto, Buddhism and Confucianism, plays a pragmatic role in creating a sense of the nation's particularistic religious identity. Religious affiliation, though, played no part in preventing adolescent delinquency (i.e., through youth groups, etc.) in Minami or Hoku. The youths I interviewed did not identify with any religious organizations nor were any of them involved in religious activities. The only adult-sponsored youth organization outside of school that played a part in the lives of these young people was the Boy and Girl Scouts, and these only had middle working class Minami youths and their middle and upper class Hoku contemporaries as members.

Given the lack of positive alternatives, it is not difficult to understand how lower working class Minami students were readily recruited into the anti-school subculture at middle school. Here, for the first time, students were expected to study hard in preparation for entrance into high school and, unlike the elementary schools, the local middle schools did not educate their students in a nurturing, egalitarian way. At the same time, students were undergoing the physical and psychological changes engendered by the onset of adolescence. As such, they were becoming more inclined to rebel against adult authority and began to refer to their peer group rather than their family as a source of identity and as the dominant influence on their behavior (Erickson 1978). In Minami, the student population became split between middle working class student's (predominantly conformists) who utilized their relative class advantage to achieve good academic results, and lower working class students (mostly non-conformists) who, due to their class disadvantages, generally achieved poor academic grades.

It was in middle school, then, that the labeling of Minami youths began. It was at this Place that Others, such as teachers, noted student behavior and academic achievement and began 'pinning' the tag of conformist/normal on some students and non-conformist/deviant on others.

The past misbehavior of lower working class students established the anti-school subculture in the Minami middle school and created an expectation that students from that sub-class would be involved in deviant activities. Letendre (2000) reported that Japanese middle school teachers held a stereotypical view that students from single-parent homes and/or of a low social-economic status were the most likely candidates for anti-social school behavior and delinquency (119–120, 135–139). Thus, it seems highly likely that teachers at the Minami middle school anticipated poor schoolwork and trouble among lower working class students, an expectation that merely reinforced the identity of the school's anti-school subculture.

Conformists at the school kept themselves separate from anti-school Actors, thereby excluding them from joining their circle of friends and engaging in conforming or conventional youth behavior. Their exclusion from the conformist group helped the non-conformist students to identify themselves as such. In other words, conformists and non-conformists have a symbiotic relationship; without one there cannot be the other. If deviance were the norm, then to conform would, paradoxically, be deviant.

While direct school actions taken against non-conforming students further stigmatized student deviant behavior, bringing police into the school did the most damage. More troublesome students are scolded or counseled at school and, in serious cases, parents are informed of their child's non-conformity and brought to the school to discuss the matter. However, given the large number of non-conforming students at the Minami middle school, and that at times things got out of hand (see Chapter 2), there was not much the teachers could do to quell student rebellion. Feeling that they were losing control, the school authorities called in the police. This, though, was then reported in the newspapers and resulted in an official, public statement decrying the students' deviant behavior. This provided perfect fodder for the already large and active delinquency prevention organizations in and around Minami and stimulated a more intensive crackdown on youth deviance. The net results was an increase in youth-adult conflict, greater cross generation suspicion and a heightening of the 'stigma' attached to students of the school.

Furthermore, such action sent a message to the students that the school authorities felt threatened by them. Students became more aware of the now officially labeled 'happenings' in the school and realized that the school authorities held them in very low esteem. This, then, was how 1st year Minami middle school students were introduced to deviant-prone situations upon their entry into adolescence.

In contrast, there were no anti-school groups in the middle schools attended by Hoku youth. With very few exceptions, whether at the local or private middle schools, Hoku students were conformists. Also, unlike in Minami, gender differentiation began at middle school. About half of Hoku's middle school students attended private, single-sex middle schools, all of which were connected to affiliated high schools. Class backgrounds of Hoku students and area privileges meant that, unlike their Minami peers, none of them entered a middle school environment that was conducive to deviant behavior.

Participation in deviant behavior

A characteristic of deviant behavior among lower working class Minami middle school students was that it did not differ according to gender. In fact, there was little gender difference in conforming behavior among middle working class Minami middle school students. Activities and behavior only varied between the conformists and non-conformist (anti-school) groups. This, then, simplified the labeling process, so that lower working class and middle working class became opposed pivotal categories each with a different set of correlative categories that define 'what they are like' (Lofland 1969: 124–126).

Humans categorize each other by nationality, gender, race, class, occupations and so on, attaching connotations or stereotypes about people that belong to such categories. Amongst the many categories assigned and tagged on to us, one usually stands out in relation to Others. Lofland states:

> For public purposes and on occasion of face-to-face engagement, one of the clustered categories is singled out and treated as the most important and significant feature of the person or persons being dealt with. It is seen as defining the character of those animals who are so clustered. That is there comes to be a pivotal category that defines "who this person is" or "who those people are" (1969: 124).

Relative to deviance, this takes the form of focusing on the social identification of Actors in order to justify and support claims that s/he is a 'certain type,' one inclined to engage in given kinds of deviant behavior. Lower working class became a pivotal category associated with various forms of youth deviant behavior or deviance that made those youth different from others deemed to be 'normal' (Lofland 1969: 121–145).

It would be harder to associate deviance to the pivotal category of lower working class youths if higher-class adolescents were equally involved in anti-school sub-cultural groups. The stigma attached to deviant behavior would then be more ambiguous because rebellious or non-conforming behavior would also be associated with youth from a middle class pivotal category, or from so-called respectable families. If this were the case, it is likely that definitions of misbehavior (smoking, drinking, truancy, etc.) would be questioned and the parameters of acceptable youth behavior expanded or seen as rather innocuous youthful deviant acts associated with growing up.

That anti-school groups were exclusively comprised of lower working class youths meant that the pivotal category of being 'lower working class' became associated with deviance; the deviant behavior of members of this grouping could then be attributed to negative characteristics of being 'lower working class.' As such, 'bad kids' might be thought of as the products of lowly educated parents, broken homes, poverty or the lowly status of their parents' occupations. This in turn creates an expectation that lower working class youths are inclined to behave in a deviant manner and will perform poorly at school; Others, then, prejudge the behavior of such youths. The converse also applies, so that middle working class youths were not expected to behave in a deviant manner and were instead extended trust by Others. If they did misbehave it was seen as an aberration, something not reflective of their character and social situation.

Anti-school subcultures are not comprised of a single group, some large, unified gang, but rather are made of a number of different friendship groups, all members engage in rebellious behavior and do substandard school work. The important point here is that for lower working class Minami youths a history of deviant behavior had been set for them prior to their entry into middle school. Nearly every lower working class Minami youth, after having completed middle school, reported that they and their best friends (who were invariably also lower working class) engaged in the same rebellious behavior at a middle school age. A precedent for student rebellion had been established, so that upon entering middle school there was a cognitive awareness of an anti-school sub-cultural group way of student behavior and Others (i.e., peers) were available as a reference group or to instruct new students in the ways of deviant behavior. It didn't matter which middle school friendship group a student belonged to the Place offered the potential for the onset and escalation of deviant behavior.

Members of anti-school subculture groups hung-out at game centers, dated, smoked cigarettes, drank alcohol and were truants. The more rebellious ones had sex, inhaled paint thinner, were violent towards others and became affiliated with youth gangs. In contrast, conformist middle school students did not engage in such rebellious behavior. They spent their time in conventional school clubs or adult-sponsored adolescent activities (such as girl scouts, private piano lessons, etc.) and studied at a *juku* or with a private tutor.

Activities and Others associated with Places outside of school followed the same lines as the characteristics of conforming and non-conforming behavior in school that separated the two student groups. Being cut off from conventional situations and activities reinforced the deviant behavior of lower working class youths and encouraged them to take on a deviant identity as non-conformists. Whether in reaction to being excluded from conventional activities or by preference, these youths hung-out at Places (entertainment districts, neighborhood hide-outs, etc.), reputably frequented by deviant youths, Places that offered further opportunities for them to misbehave and to identify with similarly disaffected Others.

Participation in deviant behavior and the adoption of a deviant identity was aided by school and community forms of delinquency control. The main function of middle schools is to sort out students for entrance into differently ranked high schools. This system of channeling students contributes to class division and the subsequent conforming or non-conforming behavior of students. Unlike in elementary school, in middle school one's grades (e.g., 2nd and 3rd year), yearly achievement test results and school behavior determine the ranking of the high school for which the teacher recommends a student to enter. For lower working class youths, joining the anti-school subculture at middle school was a defiant reaction to this 'sorting out' system; a recognition that they could not compete with higher-class students.

The school was a convenient place for the formation of peer groups. Attending school six days a week meant youths spent a lot of time at the one Place, meeting with like-minded Others. Many of the students I interviewed said that being with their best friends was the thing they liked most about middle school. Thus, peer groups were formed at middle school and were divided between conformists and non-conformists.

The local middle school was a short walk from Minami. Student behavior was not just closely monitored within the school but also beyond its boundaries, with the Hardware of the school uniform making students easily detectable in the wider community. Numerous complaints about the appearance and behavior of middle school students were made by adults, usually neighbors, associated with delinquency prevention organizations such as the Youth League (*seishōnenkai*) and Minami Crime Prevention Association (*bōhankai*) (Yoder 1986: 86–90). Some adults were determined to put a stop to such aberrant middle school student behavior as girls putting on earrings after leaving the school or boys smoking at a shrine. They called for more adult control, more punitive actions against students at school, in the home and in the community. This negative delinquency prevention approach labeled the dress and behavior of middle school students as 'bad,' which gave them all the more reason to misbehave (e.g., if this is what they expect, why not do it) and reinforced their identities as 'bad kids.'

Most of the lower working class parents felt at best ambiguous about school and the delinquency control measures that directly or indirectly affected their children. Such parents were usually aware that their children were out having fun instead of studying, but this did not create conflict in their homes. Lower working class parents did not blame their children for failing to live up to middle class adult standards of youth behavior because of the differences in class cultures. Since both parents worked in these families, or there was only a single parent and he or she worked, they had no time to get involved with school and delinquency control programs. Also, the parent(s) of students involved with the anti-school subculture in middle school had a low level of education, which not only inhibited their ability to help their children with their schoolwork, but also suggests that they too were rebellious in their youth. Not one Minami youth involved in the anti-school subculture mentioned there being conflict at home because of poor school achievement and deviant behavior. Thus, it seems these parents accepted the fates of their children and did not make an issue of it.

To participate in deviant behavior and be inscribed by Others as a deviant student in middle school was to guarantee your entry into a low ranked high school. As we have already seen, low ranked high schools are places where students with a past history of academic underachievement and behavior troubles, in short, students with a history of non-conformity, are grouped together. Although it varies in degree, all these schools have reputations for being Places of misbehavior, schools where the students are not so bright. However, the school personnel, or Others, have histories of conformity, since adults in charge of students (teachers, school counselors, etc.) all possess at least a college degree and have demonstrated their allegiance to the middle class values upheld by the education system.

Escalation into deviant roles and a deviant identity was integral to this special arrangement whereby 'school misfits' were channeled into the same schools and intensified Others expectations and labeling of Actor as a pivotal deviant student. Whereas in middle school, lower working class within the school was a pivotal category associated with youth deviance, at low ranked high schools, all students regardless of class were put into a pivotal category or more precisely belonged to a pivotal deviant student category. A pivotal student deviant category came to define 'who these youth are' more than anything else. Others associated pivotally deviant students with a set of other consistent stereotypical correlative categories such as troublemakers, delinquents, youth gang members, students who lack common social sense, school failures and so on.

Low ranked high schools present the perfect formula for maximizing the imputation of a deviant identity, with a clear split existing between persons defined as 'normal' and those defined as 'deviant,' with the 'normal' people (mainly teachers) wielding power and having control over the 'deviants' (i.e., students) (Lofland 1969: 159). Others (teachers) have reference to student records, which are submitted upon a student's application to the school. These records detail past poor school performance and behavioral problems, thereby furthering the selective perception of Others in the imputation of deviance on students.

Hardware plays a major part in the imputation of deviance at low ranked high schools. The uniforms of 'bad' schools carry a stigma and label their wearers as 'bad kids' in the public eye. Over and above this, strict rules stipulate how a uniform must be worn, which, along with rules governing hairstyles, bodily accessories, appropriate personal items, etc, are designed to regulate and inhibit a student's 'individual identity.' The students' wear of the school uniform and enforced codes of bodily appearance underlines the relative liberty accorded to the school's adult personnel. They stand out in rank and status free to wear individualized, formal civilian clothes, to choose their own hairstyle, to carry a briefcase or 'teacher looking' handbag and, in the case of female staff, to wear their own choice of make-up and jewelry.

Places, Others and Hardware are quite different for students at higher ranked high schools, a difference that increases with each incremental rise of school rank. The reputations of these Places varies from schools where 'typical students' study for college entrance to schools where the brightest students in the nation study hard in order to enter Tokyo University or one of the top private universities (e.g., Keio, Waseda or Hitotsubashi). A positive school perception of students is reflected in flexible school regulations (except at all-girls schools) that allow for 'individual identity' and promote a sense of trust between students and the school. Others in such schools (particularly those in private, higher-ranked single-sex schools) have similar area and family backgrounds, which reinforces a sense of class identity synonymous with achievement and conformity to adult and educational middle class values and standards of youth behavior. The teachers, too, share the same social class background and middle class values. Unlike lower ranked high schools, the Hardware of the school uniform for these schools signifies achievement and, in the case of upper ranked high schools, an elitist status.

The combination of Places, Others and Hardware influences how an Actor's (i.e., a student's) behavior is perceived. The school's reputation and the 'label' associated with its school uniform constantly reminds Others what 'sort' of students attend the school. For low ranked schools, suspicion, mistrust and a 'looking down' on students are not uncommon attitudes exhibited by imputation specialists. At higher ranked high schools (Places occupied by conforming or even elite students) imputation specialists expect to trust, like and even admire their students.

Differing teacher attitudes towards and selective perceptions of students means that the same student actions are often interpreted and responded to differently depending on whether they occur at a low ranked or a higher ranked high school. For example, students gathered together in a hallway at a low ranked high school are likely to be thought of by Others as being 'up to no good,' while at an upper ranked high school the same gathering would be perceived as sociable behavior. Imputation specialists expect and therefore look for 'student trouble' at low ranked high schools, but not at higher ranked high schools. This serves to foster deviant behavior at lower ranked high schools and reinforces the students' perception of themselves as misfits. Students generally meet the expectations that Others (both teachers and peers) have of them. That teachers at lower ranked high schools are always on the lookout for misbehavior also increases the probability of students being caught misbehaving, that then leads to them being counseled or expelled, thereby further entrenching their deviant identity.

Activities and places visited outside of school varied dramatically between the students at low and higher ranked high schools. As we have seen, students at higher ranked high schools were heavily involved in conventional adolescent activities while students at low ranked high schools were not. The behavior of members of anti-school subculture groups at low ranked high schools was like that of adults, but was considered deviant behavior for youths. They worked part-time, dated, smoked, drank alcohol, frequented drinking establishments, played *pachinko*, stayed out late and often were sexually active. The more defiant adolescents went beyond the boundaries of normative behavior even for adults and inhaled paint thinner, caused public disturbances, exhibited violent behavior, associated with youth gangs and committed theft.

Their attempt to redefine their student deviant identity by acting 'grown-up' meant shedding student Hardware (e.g., school uniform etc.) whenever possible, since the school uniform reminded them and Others of their 'student misfit' status. Also, when frequenting drinking establishments, they would not wear their uniforms because this alerted Others to the fact that they were minors. Only personal Hardware could provide such youths with a sense of pride and belonging, even though their chosen attire often identified them with a certain youth gang or loosely defined youth lifestyle. In contrast, students at higher ranked high schools felt pride in wearing their school uniform. They wore it longer and more often. Involvement in conventional activities meant that they wore their uniforms even after school was out, sometimes even on Sundays, when they participated in school club activities.

Class ecology greatly influenced what Lofland (1969: 138) called 'circumstances of surveillance' or the amount of time imputation specialists spent looking for and identifying instances of deviant behavior. Lower working class Minami youths were subjected to far more surveillance from middle school onwards than were higher class Hoku contemporaries. And even when Hoku youths were caught misbehaving, the consequences of it were far less serious.

Chambliss found a similar situation in his excellent 1975 fieldwork on delinquency of American lower and upper-middle class boys. While the two groups of boys were active in youth crime, only the lower class boys got caught and punished for their delinquency. Adults anticipated 'trouble' from lower class boys and were therefore attuned to the possibility of it occurring. Isolated and 'tagged' as youth deviants, the behavior of lower class boys came under close scrutiny by adults at school and in the neighborhood. This brought them into conflict with adult social control agents and eventually led to them living much less successful adult lives than their higher-class counterparts.

Two upper class Hoku boys (see Chapter 5) were rebellious and misbehaved as much as lower working class Minami youths. Their area circumstances and family class advantages, though, meant that their misbehavior led to very different outcomes than those experienced by Minami youths. One of these higher-class boys hit his teacher in middle school. His parents were notified and he apologized for his action. Nothing else was made of the matter and despite him achieving below average grades he still progressed to a middle-ranked high school. While he continued to misbehave as a high school student, his schoolwork improved and he experienced no further troubles at school.

The other upper class boy reported nine acts of misbehavior, most of which began in his last year of middle school and first year of high school. He cared little for his middle ranked high school, so had fun with his friends, smoking and playing truant. When the school authorities caught him doing these things they merely gave him a warning. This had little impact on the rest of his school life. In fact, he managed to avoid getting in any more trouble at school, mainly because the school was not strict and his schoolwork was of a good standard.

Although hitting a teacher and being caught smoking and playing truant are quite serious student offenses, these school violations and all the other acts of misbehavior committed by these upper class boys had no impact on the course of their future lives. Both boys were born and raised in a higher-class neighborhood, came from upper class families, went to a good middle school and then progressed to a higher ranked high school. They got away with their misbehavior because of the absence of strict adult delinquent controls in Hoku and the leniency extended to upper class students at higher ranked high schools. In the eyes of Hoku's imputation specialists their misbehavior was seen and treated as a passing 'adolescent thing.' As a result, both boys were not forced to exit adolescence after high school graduation, but instead were allowed to continue to study and eventually to graduate from four-year colleges.

Exiting adolescence

In this context, leaving adolescence and entering adulthood is not a fixed phenomenon, something that occurs at a predetermined age, but rather occurs when a youth enters the world of adults, at the end of their formal education. Of the youths I interviewed, the earliest this occurred was, for three of them, upon graduating from middle school and for another when he was expelled from high school. All four (one girl and three boys) actively misbehaved, three were associated with a youth gang during their time at middle school and all the boys had been officially sanctioned for having committed youth crimes. These cases provide an insight into how adult controls quickly channel non-conformists away from the mainstream of society. In one case, this led to a career in juvenile delinquency and later a deviant adult lifestyle.

The situation regarding Others was different for a Hoku girl at middle school compared to that of two Minami boys and a Hoku boy who attended a middle school outside of Hoku, one similar to the Minami middle school. For Yuki (see Chapter 4), there was no anti-school subculture at her middle school. Still, family circumstances and her contempt for school conformity facilitated early rebellion and self-recognition that she was quite different from other Hoku students.

Like almost everyone else I interviewed, Yuki, liked elementary school. She didn't, however, like middle school. Being something of a free spirit, Yuki couldn't stand middle school regulations and the teachers bodily inspections of students. She was scolded by teachers on numerous occasions for violating school rules, for example, making a mockery of the school uniform by wearing very long skirts. Yuki objected to teachers keeping a personal record on students that they then used against them. In the end, she only just managed to graduate from middle school. Yuki stood out among Hoku students not just because of her deviant ways but also because both her parents were deaf, a categorical condition that could be added by Others to her pivotal deviance package. As an outsider in Hoku, and in the absence of an anti-school subculture with which she could join, Yuki made friends with older youths that lived deviant lifestyles outside of the local school and community.

Others (teachers and students alike) labeled Yuki as 'different.' She neither fitted in nor liked school, she defied school controls and, at the young age of fifteen, graduated from middle school and entered the world of adults as a full-time waitress in a restaurant. Despite being cut-off from middle class job opportunities, Yuki has done fairly well for herself. When we last met, she was married to a cook and, together with their two children, they all lived at her parent's home in Hoku.

At the time of the original research, Yuji (see Chapter 4) had recently moved to Hoku from a community similar to Minami and he too was very isolated. Quite rebellious and an active member of a *bōsōzoku* gang, Yuji made an interesting statement regarding imputation specialists. He felt that only adults who had been in trouble as youths could understand him. He had a negative attitude toward imputation specialists (e.g., teachers and police) and disregarded their advice regarding 'normal' behavior. The more they tried to 'set him straight' the worse things became.

Yuji's *bōsōzoku* group disliked adult authority and had the reputation among Others as a 'tough group' of boys. The group's Hardware included: their motorbikes, rough physical appearances and objects such as chains that gave them a threatening look. They frequented Places like the areas near train stations and, in the summer, vacant beach shacks, which attracted other potential or actual youth deviants, particularly girls. Under close surveillance from the police, Yuji was repeatedly arrested and officially tagged as a juvenile delinquent. All of this clearly marked him off from 'normal' Others and reinforced his deviant identity as a member of *bōsōzoku*. Yuji went on to lead a deviant adult lifestyle, constantly changed jobs, was divorced and, when last contacted, was doing what is, at best, unconventional adult work.

Two Minami middle school graduates, Michio and Seiji (see Chapter 4) had similarly early exits from adolescence. The difference being that they came from poor families in a working class community where youth deviance was commonplace. They were best friends and both belonged to the anti-school subculture at their middle school. Neither boy had any intention of going to a high school.

Michio was the eldest of eight children, all of whom lived with both parents in a very cramped, run-down apartment. His father was a truck driver and both his parents just hoped he would complete his compulsory education (i.e., middle school) and then get a job. Seiji's parents ran a butcher shop in Minami and along with his parents and sister, lived at the back of the shop. Both Michio's and Seiji's parents were not normal 'Suzukis' (conventional adults), because family circumstances and their class culture was different than, if not in opposition to, middle class culture. This, combined with the prevalence of deviant Others in Minami, meant that, unlike their Hoku contemporaries, the deviant behavior of these Minami youths did not standout from that of their peers in the community. Yuki's parents' physical disability and Yuji's recent arrival in the area and his police record marked them both as outsiders in Hoku. Having been cut-off from mainstream society and exiting adolescence at the age of fifteen, Michio and Seiji quickly discovered that the smoking and drinking that had been considered deviant behavior for youths was now normal behavior for their fellow workers in the factory and mechanic's workshop in which they were now employed.

The timing of one's exit from adolescence is closely related to class, the escalation of deviant behavior and whether or not one thinks of oneself as deviant. The lower the class and the greater the division between 'normal' and 'deviant' Others (mainly achieved through the separation of students by high school rank), the earlier the exit. Adult social controls channel away potential threats to the status quo and reward conformity by delaying the exit from adolescence (via special school or college attendance) and ensure adult middle or upper class status through the social reproduction of class.

All but a small minority of low ranked high school students exited adolescence immediately after graduation. Most entered adulthood by going to work, while some Minami females entered by marrying. Most of these young people were lower working class Minami youths. By the time of their last year in high school these students were actively misbehaving, had troubles at school and most had experienced police contact. While the degree of their deviant identity varied, from youths being embarrassed to be associated with a 'bad school' through to those that identified with gangs, all recognized that Others saw them as 'student misfits.' After graduation, they continued to find themselves outside of mainstream middle class Japanese society.

Labeling youth deviance and the preservation of the status quo

Dominant group adults, utilizing their power and authority, categorize youth according to what they deem to be appropriate standards of youth behavior. The shift from an 'egalitarian,' nurturing type of primary school education to a very controlled 'militaristic' class biased secondary school education is dramatic. Adolescent Actors are subjected to the close scrutiny of imputation specialists both at school and in and around the community and may even be the subject of public imputation specialists – the mass media. The intensity of this scrutiny varies according to territory and class. The numbers of imputation specialists and selectivity of their perceptions of youth behavior increases in areas where expectations of youth deviance are highest. Minami was a Place where imputation specialists expected youths to misbehave, particularly lower working class youths, who they perceived as the most likely threats to the status quo.

The adoption of a deviant identity occurs in accordance with the following socialization dictum:

> … the greater the consistency, duration and intensity with which a definition is promoted by Others about an Actor, the greater the likelihood that an Actor will embrace that definition as truly applicable to himself (Lofland 1969: 121).

While the impact of the constant, negative labeling by Others of lower working class Minami youths as being deviant varied, it inscribed upon all of them an awareness of their misfit status. In this way, they objected to the debilitating and stigmatizing controls of teachers, police, adult delinquency prevention volunteers and even their neighbors (also see Appendix 2). The very nature of these controls, the rules and regulations that imposed limitations on the rights of youths, along with the surveillance, suspicion and mistrust, all sent a message to lower working class Minami youngsters that the imputation specialists assumed there was something seriously wrong with them. Their reasonable resentment of this attitude towards them resulted in further intergenerational conflict.

A young person's entry and participation in and exit from adolescence can be seen as an obstacle course that they must pass through to become an adult. Aged thirteen, in the first year of middle school, an adolescent is faced with a number of obstacles that s/he must successfully negotiate if s/he is to attain social economic success as an adult. The magnitude of these obstacles, though, changes depending on the adolescent's family class background and his or her place of residence. Wealthy youths from two-parent families are provided with an array of aids to help them negotiate the obstacle course, which, given their place of residence, is already relatively easy. Lower class youths, often from single-parent families, have to tackle a much harder course largely unaided. Failure to conquer each obstacle results in them either exiting the course or being sent to another course, along with all the other failures; one that leads to far fewer rewards than the main obstacle course. And, whom do imputation specialists of the status quo blame for the failure of youths to perform well on this obstacle course: the participants.

Class privileges substantially increased the probability of not just entering college but also getting into the best colleges. Class homogeneity at college interconnects with class homogeneity at the workplace, which encourages and provides opportunities for 'same class' marriages. Youths identified as potential innovators or ones perceived to be disruptive to the status quo were tagged, isolated, then forced to exit this path to power and class advantage. Those who exited early were predominantly from lower working class families. The social reproduction of class was enhanced by delinquency controls and an education system that produced the very deviance that it purported to prevent, thereby reducing opportunities for social mobility.

7 Case Studies

Case studies

Case studies provide what Selltiz (et al.) called 'insight-stimulating examples' (1959: 59–65) of divergent individuals and contrasting situations that help us better understand the different perspectives of people's various social status and positions in the social structure. This chapter continues the use of labeling conflict theory and applies it to individual cases of youths making the transition from adolescence to early adulthood. These youths represent a wide range of personal characteristics, family situations, experiences of school life, involvement in deviant behavior and self-identities. At last contact, as young adults, they were all living quite different lifestyles. Still, class ecology has been a dominant force in their lives and their confrontations, or lack there of, with the social control establishment was decisive in their transition into early adulthood.

The first criteria for the selection of the following six case studies was the availability of information relating to each individual from adolescence through to early adulthood. Then, the second criteria was that each youth (with the exception of one) typifies the different class and gender situations confronting youths in Minami and Hoku. For Minami, this meant choosing three youths (two girls and a boy) from single-parent, lower working class families. For Hoku, a boy and a girl from upper class families was selected. The exception is a case in which a boy from a middle class family moved to Hoku, lived there for a few years, but never fitted in. His family had moved from a community where youth crime was common and where the boy had been a member of a youth motorcycle gang (*bōsōzoku*). This case portrays a youth's conflict with the social control establishment and tells the story of what happened to a boy that is very defiant of adult authority.

Three of the case studies had a brother or sister that was a part of the original and follow-up studies. Information gained from these siblings is included in order to build-up a sense of the subject's character and to put into context and deepen our sense of their lives. Such information also operated as a way of cross checking the information provided by each case study. As in previous chapters, each youth and now young adult has been given a fictitious name in order to protect their privacy.

Minami case studies

Akiko Mochizuki

When I first interviewed Akiko Mochizuki in 1984 she was a third year middle school student. We met another three times that year and had a short talk each time. More than fourteen years later, in 1998, Akiko completed and returned a lengthy (63 questions) follow-up questionnaire. In March 1999, she and her elder sister (who was also interviewed in the original study and returned both follow-up questionnaires) agreed to be interviewed at their mother's house in Minami. On that occasion we sat around for more than three hours talking about their past and present lives and anything else that happened to come up.

Akiko came from a single-parent family. Her father died when she was nine years old. She was brought up by her mother and has an elder brother and elder sister. Her late father graduated from high school, while her mother never completed high school and was a self-employed photo operator.

When Akiko entered middle school she was not on an educational course that led to college. At the time, her mother was working full-time, her elder brother worked for a small company and lived away from home, and her elder sister was attending a low ranked high school. Akiko, coming from a lower working class family, was not accorded the educational extra's (home tutor or *juku*) needed to gain entrance to a good high school. She was more or less left alone to do her home-work. As such, she was ripe for recruitment into the anti-school subculture, which she duly joined in her first year at middle school.

Akiko soon began to lead a deviant student lifestyle, one facilitated by other mischievous students and a Place (i.e., the middle school) with a bad reputation. At first, seeing third year student's pick on first year students, she was a little scared of the school. Soon, though, she made friends with other girls like her and in her first year at school became sexually involved with a third year student. While the conformists were busy with study and conventional student activities, Akiko's non-conformist friendship group of ten girls was having a wild time. As a group they were all about having fun. They did things that adults forbade young girls to do. Akiko and her friends dated, went to game centers, hung-out at fast food joints, drank cocktails and smoked at each other's homes. Some, like Akiko, were also sexually active.

Typical of Minami lower working class girls, Akiko knew in middle school that she would not be going to college. Thus, she considered marriage to be the best option for her future. Early to mature, she had her first lover at thirteen. Two years after this boy broke her heart by ending the relationship, Akiko still felt hurt by him. As a third year middle school student, she dated a lower working class boy that worked full-time during the day and went to high school at night. They talked on the phone almost every day. They went out to movies, spent time together at coffee shops and during the summer went to the beach. She often came home late at night, which her mother did not object to as long as she had been told where her daughter was going. At age fifteen, Akiko was thinking about marrying once she had finished high school.

Akiko had no troubles with teachers at middle school and said that she quite liked the school as it provided her with a Place to meet with her friends. The magnitude of the anti-school sentiment at Akiko's middle school meant that the imputation specialists (teachers and school counselors) were merely attempting to avoid outright student rebellion. The non-conformist behavior of students such as Akiko was nothing remarkable and was merely an individual expression of a much larger anti-school movement. Educationally left to fend for herself, Akiko did just enough schoolwork to graduate from middle school and gain entrance to a low ranked, commercial high school in Shonan.

Akiko's sister did not like her low ranked high school and felt that the teachers didn't care about the students. She was not proud of the school. She still felt this way when we talked in 1999 and added that she, like many other students, felt the school served no purpose because it was not preparing her for college entrance exams.

Akiko, too, did not care much for her low ranked high school, though she took part of the blame, admitting that she made little effort to study and, like most of her fellow students, was too apathetic to conform to the school's expectations of students. As she had in middle school, she joined in with other anti-school students in the school, which led to an escalation of her deviant behavior.

As with her response to middle school, Akiko's rebelliousness in high school was motivated more by her feeling at odds with the adult social control establishment than by her having a particular dislike for the school or its teachers. In her first year at high school she was sometimes truant and frequented drinking establishments and other places off-limits to youths. In appearance and attitude she was 'hip' and was counseled at school for not wearing the school uniform properly and for wearing young fashionable jewelry. As with other 'hip' Minami youths, Akiko also had contact with the police. One time she was stopped when riding her motorcycle on the suspicion that she had stolen it. After showing proof of ownership, the police let her go.

Despite knowing that they were looked down on, not all students at a school like Akiko's took on the identity that Others imputed to them. Lofland made this point when he wrote:

> We should expect to find, as we indeed do, that only a small proportion of Actors who live under some deviant label actually believe they are "really" an instance of the imputed type. Apparently few youths regarded as juvenile delinquents by many others conceive of themselves in those terms (1969:189)

Akiko did not have a self-image as a '*furyō shōnen*' (delinquent youth) or 'bad girl.' In fact, a lot of lower working class Minami students, some even more rebellious than Akiko, did not think of themselves as being bad because of the non-middle class way of life imbedded in working class culture. What labeling did do to Akiko, however, was influence her thinking as an adult about youth rebellion. Just like her mother, who had not been overly concerned about her daughter's rebellious, teenage ways, now, as a married woman with a small child, Akiko thinks that misbehavior is no 'big thing,' that it's just a way of growing up. She does not agree with all the fuss adults make about trying to control adolescents. Young people, she says, need space.

With few career prospects after high school graduation, Akiko's main pursuit was to find a good husband. She worked at various part-time jobs and studied English conversation. Her middle and high school friendships continued and she made new friends amongst her fellow students at the English language school. She continued to have fun and often traveled with her friends. She dated different men and finally met her future husband, in a bank where they were both employed.

Akiko's elder sister married soon after graduating from high school and when last we met, in the spring of 1999, she had two children, one in Grade 2 and the other in Grade 5 in elementary school. Her husband also was also from a working class family. A high school graduate, he works as a truck driver and construction worker. They live in Shonan and often go back home to Minami where her elder brother, his wife and children all live with their mother.

Akiko has always been close to her mother. One reason a 'bad girl' identity did not become affixed to Akiko's self-image was that her mother did not care what others thought about her daughter; she loved her just the same. Actually, the way Akiko was raised was in contravention of the middle class values of achievement and conformity expressed through the rigidity of Japanese secondary schools. Rather, she was given freedom and enjoyed a warm, open and trusting relationship with her mother. When we met in 1999, Akiko mentioned that her mother had only two rules for her children, but that these rules were very important. Firstly, her children had to be honest. Her mother said she could accept whatever they said or did as long as they told the truth about it. And secondly, the children were to keep no secrets from her. As a result, mother and daughter remained close. In 1999, pregnant with a second child, Akiko often took her three years old daughter back home to visit her grandmother.

Akiko is the only lower working class Minami youth that I know of that is from a single parent-family and has only a high school education that married a college graduate. This, no doubt, is in part because she is a very attractive and vivacious young woman. Her husband, a college graduate, left his job at the bank, where they first met, and now works as a systems engineer. Akiko says that they get along fairly well and that her husband has become more involved in the relationship since the birth of their daughter.

Akiko is testament to a variation of the old adage, 'You can take the boy out of the country, but you can't take the country out of the boy.' Even though she has moved up the social-economic ladder, at heart Akiko remains a lower working class girl. Along with her husband and daughter, she now lives in a middle class neighborhood, but she does not like it there because she says the neighbors are cold-hearted and do not care about anyone else. Only in Minami can Akiko truly be herself. She has remained close to the working class friends she made during her middle and high school days. Although quantitative statistics would count her as upwardly mobile, she will raise her children just as her mother raised her. Such is the nature of class culture.

Nobuo Watanabe

Aged 14, in his second year at the local middle school, Nobuo was the youngest person I interviewed in Minami at the time of the original study. Later, as a second year high school student, he completed and returned the first follow-up questionnaire. Then, in 1998, eleven years after the first-follow-up, he filled out and returned a very lengthy (63 questions) questionnaire. As a result, I have a record of his transition from a middle school young adolescent, through his time as a high school student, then on into his early adulthood.

Nobuo is one of the few lower working class Minami youths that did not become part of the anti-school subculture. He liked sports, especially baseball, and associated with other students that were also into sports. Also, Nobuo had an ambition to be a train driver and this kept him out of trouble because to become a train driver one has to be able to demonstrate a history of conforming behavior.

Nobuo's father died when he was in the third year of elementary school. His father had not graduated from high school. Nobuo's mother had graduated from a special school (also called trade or specialist school) and worked full-time as a cook at a nursery school. She raised Nobuo and his elder brother by herself, while working full-time.

After middle school graduation, Nobuo entered a middle ranked high school in Shonan. At first, he liked the school and got on well with the teachers. The school wasn't strict and Nobuo kept out of trouble and did good schoolwork. After second year, however, Nobuo became less attached to the school. In the second-follow-up questionnaire he mentioned that he hated the school. He said he was not proud of the school because there was nothing to be proud about. Unlike most of his fellow students, Nobuo was not being prepared for college (a college education was not a prerequisite for becoming a train driver) and as a result of this lack of motivation the standard of his schoolwork fell to be below average.

Nobuo's participation in deviant youth behavior began later than for most other Minami lower working class youths. This was largely because he was a conformist in middle school and therefore did not attend a low ranked high school. Typically for a Minami student at higher ranked high schools, his misbehavior was more an adventurous activity than part of a collective act of defiance against adult authority. At fifteen Nobuo stayed out late at night without parental approval and at sixteen drank alcohol and read a pornographic magazine.

Nobuo has always got along well with his mother. When in middle school, he said that, for the most part, they had a trusting relationship. Atypical for lower working class parents, his mother stressed the need to succeed academically and, although she was not very strict, they had minor squabbles about his study habits. Nobuo recognized his mother's good qualities and said that he wouldn't mind being like her when he grew up, though he preferred to be his own person.

In high school, Nobuo was still close to his mother and they talked about many things together. Eleven years later, as a young adult, Nobuo and his mother continued to get along well. She trusted and understood him and he felt very close to her.

After high school graduation, Nobuo found work in the public transport network. By 1998 he had fulfilled his dream and was working as a train driver. He was married with two children, liked his job and had a good relationship with his wife. In the second follow-up study, Nobuo noted that he and his wife trust, respect and understand each other well. He also said that his family and job were the two most important things in his life.

Nobuo and Akiko had much in common. Both came from a lower working class, single-parent family and both enjoyed a very close relationship with their mothers. There was, however, one major difference: Nobuo had a career goal that he fulfilled, whereas Akiko was not given that option. While it did not matter to Akiko which high school she attended, for Nobuo it was important that he gained entry to a middle-ranked high school. His desire to attend such a school deterred him from getting involved in anti-school activities while at middle school. Neither

Akiko nor Nobuo really liked their high school, but Akiko's dislike was more of rebellion fostered by her low ranked school's anti-school subculture, something that was absent from Nobuo's middle ranked school.

Nobuo, then, was an exception to the general rule exemplified by Akiko that the decision to join a conformist or non-conformist peer group in middle school was closely connected to the student's family class background. Gender, though, also played a role. Lower working class boys like Nobuo, those with a high school education, have a better chance of establishing a career for themselves than do their female counterparts. Thus, they have greater incentive to resist joining the anti-school subculture in middle school, for to do so is to jeopardize their future career prospects. This also results in greater financial and emotional investment being made in the education of boys than that of girls; a fact reflected in the disproportionate number of males compared to females that attend four-year colleges (Reischauer 1977: 210; Rohlen 1983:16). This is also supported in that the only two college graduates from Minami lower working class families were males. In this way, gender discrimination in the workplace encourages adolescent rebellion among lower class girls.

Natsumi Makino

Natsumi was a second year student at a low ranked public high school in Shonan at the time of the original study. When she completed the questionnaire for the first follow-up study she was attending an animal grooming special school. Eleven years later, by the time of the second follow-up study, Natsumi and her father (she had lived with her father) had moved without leaving a forwarding address. After much searching and some clandestine negotiations – Natsumi's father used to run a Majan (Chinese gambling) parlor in their old house and may have been in hiding from either the police or ex-clients – I finally managed to track down Mr. Makino and was able to conduct the final follow-up interview with Natsumi over the phone.

Natsumi lived alone with her father when the original interview took place. Her parents had been separated for a number of years. As already mentioned, her father was a gambling operator. Her mother lived separately and worked at a sushi shop. Later, her parents divorced.

Natsumi's situation was different from those of Akiko and Nobuo, not just because she was raised by her father and not her mother, but also because of her father's unconventional line of work. In Minami, though, this was not all that unusual, but was rather just another aspect of the area's lower working class culture; a culture that did not orient a child towards middle class conformity. Natsumi was born in Minami, all of her friends lived in or near Minami, and she found it quite easy to participate in deviant behavior in the context of the middle school's anti-school subculture.

Natsumi was a rebellious young girl. At fifteen years old she dated, went to game centers, was truant, smoked, drank alcohol and violated the curfew. At age sixteen, her first year at a low ranked high school, she was sexually active and drank alcohol at a drinking establishment. She got into trouble at high school for violating the school dress code and was also caught at a drinking party at the school that resulted in almost all the partygoers being suspended. The police questioned Natsumi for suspected truancy. However, it was actually a school holiday and she was quite upset with the police for their false accusation. On another occasion she was 'written up' for a traffic violation.

As with Akiko and Nobuo, Natsumi had a good relationship with her custodial parent. Her father trusted her. He was not at all strict and they often spent quality time together. In both the initial interview and the first follow-up study, Natsumi stated that she had a close relationship with her father. While it seems likely that his unconventional job may have had something to do with her non-conformity and her dislike for the adult social control establishment, it was the more general effect of living in Minami that led to her deviant youth behavior.

Being born and raised in Minami presents a youth with ample opportunity to enter into a peer group whose members are active in youth crime. Having joined such a peer group, an Actor is placed in a situation of 'least resistance' (Lofland, 1969: 74) as they are pressured to engage in the same deviant acts as their peers. Once Others (i.e., her friends) began smoking, drinking, being truant and so forth, it was only a matter of time before Natsumi followed their lead. This, of course, was the situation at the local Minami middle school, where the anti-school subculture complemented the unconventionality of Natsumi's family situation. From there she followed the usual course to a low ranked high school, where it would have been hard for her to find a group of peers who did not engage in acts of youth deviance.

As discussed in Chapter 3, low ranked high schools are stricter than higher ranked schools because teachers at these schools expect trouble from the students. The strictness, however, merely increases the students' resentment, that in turn increases the likelihood of their rebellion. Like many of her peers, Natsumi disliked her school's strict regulations. Both while still at the school, and later, after graduation, she complained that the teachers were serious about enforcing the school's rules. She said the only thing she liked about the school was that it gave her an opportunity to get together with her friends.

Natsumi did not think very highly of Minami adults. Neighbors, she said, didn't trust each other and she thought the neighborhood crime prevention association was a waste of time, because it did not and could not prevent delinquency. Natsumi did not like the police. She felt they were too strict with Minami youths.

That Natsumi was able to attend an animal grooming special school after graduating from high school suggests that her father had a higher income than most other lower working class Minami families. After graduating from animal grooming school, Natsumi worked at a pet shop. She soon married and had a child and, the last time we talked, in 1999, her son was ten years old and, a month earlier, she had given birth to another boy. The last I heard, she was a housewife, living near Minami in a similar working class community. Natsumi's two children will be raised in a working class environment, just like she and her sister were, although for the time being at least her children are living in a two-parent family.

Hoku case studies

Shinichiro Tajima

I first interviewed Shinichiro at my home. Three years later he completed the first follow-up questionnaire. Information for the second follow-up, in March 1999, was obtained through an interview which I conducted at his parents' home. At that time, he was single, lived at home and was working as a chiropractor.

Shinichiro is from an upper class family. His father went to Kyoto University, a prestigious national university. The family has an upper class heritage – a relative was one of the dignitaries that met Commodore Matthew Perry when he came to open Japan up to the world on the famous black ships in 1853. Another relative is a member of the National Diet. His father had retired from a company in Tokyo, and was financially well-off. In addition to retirement pay, he also gained income from his ownership of two apartment buildings. The Tajima's nice home sits between another, smaller house that they own and a work shed, all on a fairly large plot of land.

As with so many youths in Hoku, the combination of Place, Other and Hardware ensured that Shinichiro avoided becoming involved in deviant youth behavior. Shinichiro, an only child in an upper class Hoku family, was, from birth through to college, associated with Places and Others that made the onset of youth deviance very improbable. From the first grade of elementary school onwards he attended elite, private schools, all of which were within walking distance of Hoku. The private all-boys' middle school that he attended was connected to a private upper ranked all boys' high school, entrance to which was almost guaranteed. Graduating from high school, he duly went to college and then to graduate school, where he obtained a Master of Arts degree in the Sociology of Law. He later studied chiropractic medicine and, in 1999, was a practicing chiropractor.

The primary and secondary schools Shinichiro attended were composed of middle and upper class students. In effect, preparation to enter into the best universities in Japan began from first grade. He had private tutors and an Aunt helped with his English. School life was enjoyable. Proud of his high school, he received a positive identity by going there. He liked his teachers and the school was not strict.

At the time of his first year at a private, upper ranked, all-boys' high school Shinichiro reported that he had never misbehaved nor been in any sort of trouble. Later, after high school graduation, he reported two acts of misbehavior: at sixteen he read a pornographic magazine and at seventeen he drank alcohol without his parents' permission.

Shinichiro's parents were, compared to the parents of his friends, older and they were conservative in their thinking. He, too, was conservative. In the original study he was one of the few youths that said adults understood youths and that there was no generation gap. During adolescence he did not have a date. What, one might ask, did he do for fun during his secondary school days? He and his well-off friends studied together and played computer games at Shinichiro's house.

Shinichiro has always had good relationships with his parent's, especially with his mother. As the only child in a well-off family, Shinichiro led a very guarded, conservative life. One day he will inherit his parents' considerable wealth. If he marries and has a child, that child will begin life very much the way he did – cosseted by privilege.

A major turning point for Shinichiro occurred soon after he finished graduate school, when he was involved in a car accident. As part of his rehabilitation he saw a chiropractor. Impressed with the treatment he received, he decided to study chiropractic medicine, which led to his current career.

Kanako Watanabe

I knew Kanako before the original study began because we (my family – wife and two infant daughters) rented and were residing in the lower story of her parents' two-story home. Of all the members of the Watanabe family, Kanako was the one with whom I was closest. For six years, from 1981 to 1987, we met each other like family and sometimes talked. Usually, though, our encounters merely consisted of a greeting. Between my return to Japan in 1991 and the second follow-up study in 1998 and 1999, Kanako and I would sometimes meet by chance and talk together. We have always got on well together.

Kanako is from an upper class family and has always lived at home. Now married, she lives next door to her parents in a two-story house built on her parents' land. Her father, retired, worked in a managerial position for a middle-sized company in Tokyo. Her mother has never worked outside of the home and, in the past, was kept busy raising Kanako and her younger brother and sister. Both parents are college graduates. The Watanabe's have four houses on their large plot of land in Hoku, two of which they rent out.

Kanako was all but guaranteed college entrance when she entered high school. Characteristic of Hoku females, she attended an all girls' upper ranked high school in Kaigan. This high school was attached to an all girls' four-year college, which she also attended. Kanako liked high school and had nothing but good things to say about her high school and her college. Students and teachers had trusting relationships and everyone got along just fine. Quite conservative, Kanako did not date until she was seventeen years old and reported only one act of misbehavior: at eighteen she drank alcohol without her parents knowing.

Kanako's exit from adolescence was, like that of the large majority of Hoku youth, postponed by college; the only period in her adolescence in which she had enough free time to have fun. Once at college she majored in nutrition and later became a nutritionist at a hospital. She then married and, as has been mentioned, now lives next door to her parents in one of their four houses.

Her parents are not strict. She and her mother have always been close and she thinks quite highly of her father. She emulates her mother and admires her father. Kanako's father has always been a hard worker. In the past, when not away at work, he always kept himself busy in the garden or fixing up something on the block of land.

As with many Hoku females, Kanako appears to be quite formal and lady-like, but this is just the surface of her personality. If one were to meet Kanako for the first time, she would appear quiet, shy and very formal. Once you get to know her, however, she is quite open, honest and down-to-earth. Being raised in an upper class family and leading the life of a conformist has its drawbacks, as does any lifestyle. For one, Kanako has lived a very confined life, one in which she has been expected to act like a 'proper' Japanese lady.

Since marrying, Kanako has suffered from severe back pains. Both she and I feel that her back pains are the result of stress, though neither of us is sure of the source of the stress. We often talked about her back pains and about her inability to become pregnant, a situation made worse by the fact that her younger sister became pregnant soon after marrying and gave birth to a baby boy. In 2002, aged 37, Kanako remained childless.

Kanako has always been under pressure to do things in the proper manner and I suspect this might be one of the causes of her unremitting back pain. Despite her privileged upbringing, her personal life has not been all that great. While, unlike her lower working class contemporaries, she has been free of troubles with the social control establishment and has received the best education, married 'well' and has a good home life, Kanako has been under constant pressure to perform well academically and to be a model housewife. Lower working class women are not confronted with such pressures.

Kanako has been given little space and has been confined by the high expectations of Others. Her inability to bear a child has put an extraordinary strain on her life. She has nowhere to escape. In contrast, Akiko, who does not like the neighbors in her new, middle class community, regularly escapes back to Minami where she meets with her family and friends. She can get rid of her stress whereas Kanako cannot. Furthermore, Akiko feels fortunate to have married 'up,' to have attained middle class status, and is quite content to be a housewife and mother. In contrast, Kanako remains childless and, although she is a college graduate and is qualified to be a nutritionist, upper class social pressures have shackled her to the role of a model housewife and have inhibited her from pursuing her own career.

Yuji Daida

After being interviewed for the original research, Yuji agreed to meet with me again, which he did at different times and places during the few years he lived in Hoku. Twelve years later, he completed and returned the second follow-up questionnaire.

Yuji is not really a Hoku youth. He and his family moved to Hoku from an area similar to Minami when he was fifteen years old. By then Yuji had already been in a lot of trouble for deviant youth behavior. After a few years, the family moved again, away from Hoku – I suspect because Yuji was again misbehaving. Yuji's story provides an insight into what Hoku looks like from the perspective of a rebellious outsider. Yuji was in constant conflict with the adult social control establishment throughout his adolescence. The consequences of this on his adult life reveals what can happen to a youth that refuses to submit to the system of adult controls.

Growing up where he did, in a place very similar to Minami, Yuji was immersed in an equivalent deviant youth sub-culture. The degree of seriousness of his deviant behavior had a profound affect on his adult life. Unlike lower working class Minami youths, though, Yuji was actually from a middle class family. Their move to the conservative environs of Hoku, though, failed to change his deviant ways.

Yuji's family was middle class, though his parents had financial problems. He described his family as lower-middle class, because they had a loan on their house and because although his father was a college graduate he was employed as a public worker. Despite his middle class status, all of Yuji's close friends were rebellious, most belonged to the lower class and all members of a *bōsōzoku* group.

The area Yuji lived in before moving to Hoku offered him ample opportunity to misbehave. He began misbehaving in middle school, joined the *bōsōzoku* and entered a low ranked high school. Aged sixteen, he moved to Hoku and was expelled from the high school for assaulting his physical education teacher. From middle school, through his adolescence and into his early adulthood, Yuji's life was marked by conflict with adult authoritarian figures.

Yuji hung-around with a tough group of boys; he joined the *bōsōzoku* when he was fourteen years old. All ten of his gang member friends either ended their education after graduating from middle school or dropped out of high school. While still at middle school age, Yuji began smoking, drinking, playing truant, being aggressive and violent towards outsiders, and participating in gang activities. After entering and then quickly being expelled from a low ranked high school, his involvement in youth crimes escalated and he began inhaling paint thinner, drinking at bars, playing *pachinko* and had his first sexual encounter. It was at this time that he was arrested for not having a driver's license when cruising around with the *bōsōzoku*. He was also having difficulty sticking with one job and was not comfortable living in Hoku. Yuji didn't like Hoku youth because they were 'rich and stuck-up.'

The escalation of Yuji's deviant behavior and his resistance to imputation specialists labeling of him is a telling story of one youth's struggle to maintain a sense of self-respect in the face of the power of the social control establishment. Yuji was not passive, but rather resisted authority wherever he encountered it. Attempts by the adult authorities to control him failed and official labeling of him only resulted in more deviance, further police contact and his eventual isolation from mainstream society.

Yuji was loyal to his *bōsōzoku* and strongly identified with it. He did not think what the gang did was so bad. After his arrest for riding with the *bōsōzoku* without a driver's license, the police tried to persuade Yuji to 'rat' on his friends. They pressured him to tell about his involvement with the *bōsōzoku* and to provide them with the names of other group members. They tried in vain to convince him that what the *bōsōzoku* was doing was wrong. Yuji refused to succumb to their threats and remained silent even after the police hit him.

While the police perceive the *bōsōzoku* as juvenile delinquents, a menace to society, Yuji thought differently. He disliked the police, not just because they constantly harassed the *bōsōzoku*, but also because they sided with other groups that the *bōsōzoku* did not like.

Speaking of one incident, Yuji felt that *bōsōzoku* violence was sometimes a good thing. He told the story of a confrontation between a particular *bōsōzoku* group and the *aikoku dantai* (love your country group) a fanatical right-wing, Japanese nationalist group. Groups like the *aikoku dantai* often drive slowly through the main streets of cities and towns and loudly broadcast patriotic, ethnocentric messages, calling for the return of Imperial rule or blaming all of Japan's woes on foreigners polluting Japan's pure race. On this one occasion a *bōsōzoku* group attacked the *aikoku dantai* while they were broadcasting such messages. Riding their motorcycles, they came alongside the truck, swinging chains and threatening the fanatics with violence if they didn't get off the street. Yuji said that the police then got involved and protected the *aikoku dantai* and harassed the *bōsōzoku*.

Yuji dismissed the credibility of authority figures that labeled him a 'bad boy.' He thought that unless an adult had experienced the same sort of troubles in their youth as he had that they could not possibly know or understand him.

As we have seen, teacher violence in low ranked high schools is not an uncommon occurrence. And, while students didn't like this violence they generally did nothing about it. Yuji was different. Yuji's physical education teacher had hit him and his fellow students. Finally, Yuji had had enough of this physical abuse and he grabbed the teacher in a headlock. For this, he was expelled from the school.

Consequently, Yuji exited adolescence early, with a police record that, besides the driving offence, included three citations for misbehavior. Faced with the challenge of making his way in the world, the official labeling machinery (e.g., the school and police) made it difficult for Yuji to become a 'normal' adult. Certainly, his police and school record precluded him from getting a good, mainstream job. The police kept Yuji under surveillance and asked other Hoku youths in the neighborhood if they had heard any information about him, which only contributed to his 'bad boy' reputation. Cut off from employment opportunities in mainstream society, Yuji furthered his career as a juvenile delinquent. In the second follow-up study, Yuji informed me that since our first meeting he had been arrested a number of times as a juvenile for, among other crimes, assault and blackmail.

There was an admirable side to Yuji that adult authorities failed to take into account. Namely, his moral convictions that the context of an action is important and that deference to authority should not be automatic, authority figures should pay the price like anyone else for taking advantage of others. He justified '*bōsōzoku*' action against *aikoku dantai* on the grounds that these people are extreme nationalists and I may add that their attempt to stir up a racist sense of superiority is far more dangerous than any *bōsōzoku* activity. Even his attack on his physical education teacher can seem justified when one knows that this teacher abused his authority by physically striking students. Yuji also empathized with the situation of his *bōsōzoku* friends who faced difficult futures because of their low levels of education and their troubles with the police. He was quite pleased when one of his *bōsōzoku* friends quit his habit of inhaling paint thinner and got a full-time job as a carpenter.

Yuji was a complex youth. He resisted authority, but then felt remorse for the troubles he caused his parents. Having already become so deeply involved in *bōsōzoku* activities, the labeling machinery only reinforced his identity with that group and made the adoption of any alternative identity almost impossible. Conflict continued into his adult life. He married and was divorced, changed jobs often and, in 1999, was working as some kind of salesman outside of an office, a position that may well be associated with deviant adult activities.

The case studies in summary

These six cases reveal a wide range of life experiences and behaviors during the participants' transitions from adolescence to early adulthood. The interaction between class culture, Places, Others and Hardware was crucial in forming each Actor's perceptions and behavior during their adolescence and into their early adulthood. In order to study the similarities and differences of these six cases I have, in what follows, placed them in two categories: conformists and non-conformists. A brief comparison of these two groupings will sum up the circumstances of adolescence, youths' clashes with the social control establishment and the consequences of these on their lives as young adults.

As adolescents, Nobuo, Shinichiro and Kanako all led conformist lives and, as such, experienced little or no conflict with the social control establishment. Nobuo's case could be used as an example of a Japanese success story; of how a disadvantaged boy, with the aid of his single-parent mother's care and self-sacrifice and his own dedication and discipline, rose from his lower working class roots to become a solid citizen. Most adolescents in Nobuo's circumstances, though, especially girls, rebelled against the status quo. Hence, Nobuo's case demonstrates that nothing is entirely predetermined. By associating with conformist Others at middle school, Nobuo avoided stigmatized Places (e.g., a low ranked high school) that were highly conducive to the escalation of deviant behavior and the adoption of a deviant identity. Still, his lower working class background was the main reason for him not going to college and, as a train driver with a wife and two children, he remains socially very distant from the likes of Kanako and Shinichiro.

Kanako and Shinichiro led very sheltered, upper class conformist adolescent lives. Even as adults they continue to associate exclusively with people from their own class and would have no idea what life is like for a lower working class person living in an underprivileged area. Both Kanako and Shinichiro have attained a respectable occupational status, one deemed appropriate to their upper class family backgrounds. The social control establishment worked in their interest and, as expected, they have conformed to its requirements and been rewarded by the social reproduction of their upper class status.

In contrast, Akiko, Natsumi and Yuji were rebellious youths that opposed the social control establishment. They all found themselves in the same circumstances and Places conducive to the onset and escalation of deviant youth behavior. Rather than deter them from deviant behavior, adult controls facilitated it. Imputation specialists contributed to the escalation of their deviant behavior by expecting trouble from them.

Akiko and Natsumi realized that because they were youths their behavior was deemed deviant, even though the same behavior was considered perfectly acceptable when exhibited by an adult. Sensing hypocrisy, they decided there was nothing wrong with what they did. Yuji strongly identified with his *bōsōzoku* group and thought adult authorities incapable of understanding him and his fellow *bōsōzoku* members. All three youths dismissed the validity of the 'delinquent' labels that adults attempted to pin on them.

For Akiko and Natsumi, class culture guarded them against the negative labels created by the imputation specialists at school and those adults in the neighborhood active in delinquency prevention.

Feeling supported by their friends and single-parents, they didn't really care what these Others said about them. They went on to lead fairly stable adult lives, but their identities remained working class and it is this culture that they will pass on to their children.

Once Yuji began at an early age to engage in rebellious youth activities his life became one of constant conflict with adult authority. Moving to Hoku had no affect on his behavior or lifestyle. Yuji's life followed a path of crime, one well mapped by the American literature on youth crime. Kassebaum (1974) notes that the younger the age of involvement in crime and the earlier experiencing trouble with the law, the more likely a youth is to become a career criminal. Cut-off from mainstream society, Yuji continues to struggle to find a place in a society that punishes non-conformity quite severely.

8 Conclusion

Summary

This research studied the conditions and circumstances of pre-delinquency by comparing the youth crimes committed by adolescents that lived in an area conducive to delinquency with those committed by young people living in an area not considered to be delinquency-prone. Class ecology was identified as a main condition of youth deviance and, as such, was central to our understanding of the lives of the Minami and Hoku youths that were traced from early adolescence through to early adulthood. A labeling conflict perspective was then applied to the process of becoming an adult, with the focus being on the consequences of adolescent deviance to a youth's transition into early adulthood. The enormous impact and repercussions of the interaction between Places, Others and Hardware on an Actor's exposure to and participation in youth deviance, the nature of their self-identity and the timing of their exit from adolescence was central to this process of transition and the social reproduction of class.

The adult social control establishment employed imputation specialists to crack down on non-conformist adolescents that questioned the 'status quo.' This resulted in such young people being channeled away from mainstream society. Class ecology meant that it was Minami youth, rather than their Hoku contemporaries that were identified as those most likely to question the validity of adult authority to impose a set of standards for youth behavior. Consequently, disadvantaged, lower working class Minami youth were separated from middle working class Minami youth after entering the Place (i.e., middle school) where Others (imputation specialists, mainly teachers and adults involved in delinquency prevention) began to carefully judge, grade and sort out the conformists from the non-conformists. It was in this context that the anti-school subculture developed at the middle school, a development that resulted in widespread misbehavior and other expressions of non-conformity (poor schoolwork, hanging-out at game centers, etc.). Given the clash of class cultures played out through the education system, most members of this subculture were from the lower working class.

Putting all poor academic achievers (related to class ecology) into the same Place (low ranked high schools) wearing identifiable Hardware (school uniforms) and Others (students) of the same 'labeled' category or imputation specialists (i.e., teachers) was clearly the most dominant force in the escalation of deviant youth behavior. While such students did not necessarily see themselves as 'student misfits' in the way that their 'label' suggested, they nevertheless were all aware of their 'deviant' student status.

My initial research that began nearly twenty years ago, set out to discover whether or not living in a delinquency prone area resulted in an increased likelihood of an adolescent committing more youth crimes. As should by now be obvious, the answer to this question was, 'Yes.' The strong results regarding 'class ecological differences' were quite revealing, especially given that previous studies of crime and delinquency in Japan had overlooked the importance of area and class background on youth deviance. Results of the two-follow up studies were equally, if not more, surprising.

The original and follow-up studies revealed that younger (14 to 16 years old) Minami and Hoku youths closely followed the same pattern of adolescent behavior as their older (17 to 19 years old) peers did. This strongly suggested that the influences of class and area ecology were being replicated. The younger lower working class cohort of Minami youth went on to experience the same kinds of conflict with the social control establishment as the older lower working class Minami youths had. The younger Minami middle working class youths similarly followed their older counterparts' more conforming route through adolescence, one which led to much less conflict with the social control establishment. This social reproduction of class also extended across generations, so that both lower working class and middle working class Minami youths remained in the same class as their parents after they became adults.

The pattern was similar for the higher-class youths of Hoku. The small number of middle class Hoku youths that attended low ranked high schools, and were thereby exposed to the interaction of the same Places, Others and Hardware as those experienced by lower working class Minami youths, were similarly affected. Namely, there was an escalation of their deviant behavior, they became aware of being labeled a 'student misfit' and they generally had an early exit from adolescence.

However, the vast majority of younger middle, and all younger upper class Hoku youths led privileged, conformist adolescent lives, much like those led by the older cohort. And, again, in the higher classes, class position was socially reproduced. Put simply, the influences of area ecology, class background, class culture and the conflict with and labeling by the social control establishment were consistent facilitators over time influencing youth deviance and their course of transition into young adulthood.

Such findings shed new light on the nature of conformity in Japan. Conformity is not universal, but is class based and rather than reflecting harmony, it grows out of conflict. By blocking admission to potential troublemakers, the educational tracking system minimizes the possibility of student dissent at higher ranked high schools. It also fosters a sense of homogeneity amongst higher-class students at such schools. Demonstrated conformity then leads to college and the best, most socially influential jobs. All of this ensures the preservation of the 'status quo.'

Given that the adult criteria for youth conformity is rigidly middle class in nature, it is not surprising that there is a disproportionately large number of students from disadvantaged families that fail to live up to mainstream expectations regarding academic achievement and adolescent behavior. Permanently marked as adolescent failures and either ending their education after middle school or being bunched together at low ranked high schools, these youths are prime candidates for youth deviancy and gang activity. There are no open admission programs for either high school or college, so the whole process of taking and passing college entrance exams coincides with class privileges. Early adolescent non-conformity, which is closely related to class, is harshly dealt with by the education system, thereby almost guaranteeing that novel ideas that question the authority of established practice will ever be an acceptable part of mainstream society.

Conformity is idealized in Japan. The popular Japanese expression of *deru kugi wa utareru* (the nail that sticks out is struck down), suggests that one must not stand out from the crowd or you will be pressured to conform like everyone else (Condon, 1984: 10–11). The findings of my research, however, suggests a new, more merciless expression of conformity is at play, *deru kugi wa nukareru* (the nail that sticks out is removed) or if you don't conform as we want, you will be rejected and cast out.

Recently, I read a summary of yet another study claiming that a bad home environment is the cause of misbehavior and juvenile delinquency (Japan Times, June 2002). Over the past three decades there have been very few studies that have taken a critical look at youth crime in Japan. Most research has glaringly neglected questions of inequality (including social class and gender) and class bias in status and ranking within the educational system. Even more worrying is the fact that the role of the social control establishment in causing conflict and thereby contributing to the problem of youth crime has remained unchallenged.

Results of the escalation of adult social controls

The 1990's not only witnessed the continuation of a high juvenile arrest rate and substantially increased rates of school violence, but also a widespread apathy, bordering on contempt, among youths towards education. Today, more students than ever are flaunting school dress codes. And, while data is not available, I would suggest that such deviancy (along with arrest rates and student violence) tie in closely with social class and the educational tracking system. In other words, that such deviant behavior is most acute at troubled middle schools in lower and lower-middle working class areas and at low ranked high schools.

The national educational reforms implemented in 2002 have little to do with the real world of Japan's youth. The problems of delinquency identified by the National Education Council on Educational Reform represent conservative, middle class, adult perspectives on youth crime rather than those of the country's youth. In all likelihood, Government solutions that flow from these flawed definitions and diagnoses will only serve to make the situation worse than it already is.

These educational reforms stemmed from recommendations to the Prime Minister by, among others, the National Commission on Educational Reform advisory council. The Central Council on Education and Curriculum Council was most influential in the changes made to primary and secondary school education. To combat youth problems, in 2000 The National Commission on Educational Reform and Central Council of Education emphasized the need for a re-socialization of adolescents, at home, in the community and at school. They called for a revival of traditional Japanese values to be instilled in the country's youth, emphasizing obligation, commitment, duty and loyalty to the community and state (Japan Times, June 2000; Kreitz-Sandberg 2000).

Moral education, under the rubric of a new area of study called cross-subject learning, now begins in 4th grade of primary school and gradually increases with each school year. Other measures are being taken to get families and communities more involved in school activities. Furthermore, students will be required to perform a certain number of hours of volunteer community work.

The Ministry of Education also plans to intervene in family affairs and the ways parents raise their children. They are advocating more domestic discipline and will get involved in matters relating to parents' socialization of their child. This was clearly stated in one of the ministry's reform measures: 'we will provide families more opportunities to learn home discipline and to share experience, and promote measures to support and encourage fathers' participation in home discipline' (Kreitz-Sandberg 2000: 13).

Gender and class inequality, however, have received no attention in these sweeping national educational reforms. Amidst all these reforms, none of them is directed to bringing about a more equal access to a good education. The basic educational hierarchy remains intact and most likely will become even more class biased with the reduction in school hours. Shorter school hours is an advantage for higher class students whose parents can pay for them to receive even more private tutoring in the longer time available. Saito felt that such changes will result in an even greater disparity in education between the classes, forcing the middle and upper classes to attend private schools free from government restraints, while leaving the public schools to the lower classes.

> The implications are clear. The children of wealthy families will grow up attending private schools and studying hard. They will advance in life to the limit of their talent and effort. They are expected to apply themselves to studying in an environment of free competition. Less well-off children, many of them condemned to mediocrity, will learn the basics of reading and writing and computer use, and that will have to be enough for them. (2001: 27–28)

Susanne Kreitz-Sandberg, a leading expert on national education reform measures, recognized that the voice of youth was not heard when these educational reforms were being made.

> Having spent a considerable time reading documents published by various councils appointed by the Ministry of Education, I can not withstand the strong impression that the Reform failed to grasp the real changes in the reality of the adolescents (2000:17)

McVeigh (2000) wrote that all post-war educational reforms instigated by the state have been conservative and elitist. Real educational reforms, ones that would benefit the majority, are not considered, let alone implemented, because many in influential positions are satisfied with the 'status quo,' with the education system operating like a service industry for the nation-state and corporate sector. McVeigh argues that citizen-based educational reforms are unlikely to come about because, 'rather than the state/capital nexus existing for the sake of citizens, the citizens and society are working hard to benefit the state' (2000: 89).

Necessary changes

While it is unlikely that the present, hierarchical education system is going to change any time soon, small changes within its existing structure could be easily made immediately. The following are some suggestions for such changes, ones that might improve the inequality and mitigate youth-adult conflict.

A school uniform attaches a label to every student that wears one. Students are required to wear them on their way to and from school. Most people in the local community recognize the different high school uniforms worn by students in their area. The reputation and image of these schools is attached to the students wearing the uniform and others treat them according to the reputation of the uniform they are wearing.

The school uniform sets students apart, distinguishing students from a low ranked high school from those attending a high ranked school. For students at low ranked high schools, putting on their school uniform is like wearing a badge labeled 'student misfit.' Students at such schools often wear their uniforms so as to mock them. For example, the boys wear their pants extremely low and only button half their shirt and the girls wear their skirts extremely high or wear conspicuous shorts underneath them. Many of these students also have perm and bleached hair and pierced body parts. Through these gestures of defiance they are saying, 'Here is what you can do with your uniform and school dress code.'

The stigma attached to attending a low ranked high school could be reduced if school uniforms were either abolished all together or if all students were made to wear the same school uniform. If either of these policies were adopted at public high schools they would set a precedent that the private schools might feel pressured to follow. Similarly, other school regulations and student codes of conduct should be looked into to provide a more egalitarian treatment of students regardless of their high school rank.

Apathy and rebellion characterizes school life for students at low ranked high schools. Feeling rejected by the education system, they know they have little prospect of having a respectable career. This, though, need not be the case. Okano and Tsuchiya (1999) found a significant difference between student behavior at low ranked agricultural high schools that existed in name only with no consideration given to eventual work in agriculture and that of the students at agricultural schools that genuinely prepared their students for a career in agriculture. The former students were ashamed of their schools and reacted by misbehaving, while the latter students were attached to and proud of their schools and were not at all rebellious. In other words, students need a reason to study and one way to provide them with one is for them to attend trade, or special schools that prepare them for a specific career or job.

Low ranked high schools could be either affiliated with a special school or have a curriculum that prepared students for a special school of their preference. These special schools need to be affordable for lower working class students, with financial assistance given to those who need it.

Females from lower class families are the most disadvantaged of all students, since the best jobs (for example, public and private transportation work, blue-collar jobs, etc.) that require only a high school education are restricted to males or, at the very least, are extremely hard for females to attain. Also, promotional opportunities for women regardless of educational attainment at white-collar jobs are limited. Hence, female students need to be given more job and career opportunities. To this end, the large number of all-girls schools, especially junior colleges, that seem to only prepare females for a life of being a housewife and mother need to change their curricula so that their students are oriented towards their own job interests and careers.

College entrance exams do not fit the present times. Japan is an aging society with fewer young people entering college than any time in the postwar period. This dwindling college population is now requiring colleges to downsize or even close and the situation is projected to get worse. A more open college admission policy, one that allows all high school graduates of any age a chance to enter would help reverse this trend. It would also serve to dilute the class elitism prevalent in colleges and bring a greater range of ages, social experiences and minority group representation into the universities. Financial and school assistance programs are needed for lower class students, ethnic minorities (Ainu, Koreans, Chinese, Filipinos, Southeast Asians, South Americans and Middle Easterners), offspring of a Japanese and foreign parent (labeled and called *hafu* in Japanese meaning half-breeds) and Burakumin.

Future research

For over thirty years adults have increased their social controls over youths without attempting to really understand the world of adolescence. Youths have been judged according to the conservative and often anachronistic adult standards of an older generation. Those that have had the most power to initiate, implement and carry out control measures over youths have predominantly been older, higher-class males. The conservative Liberal Democratic Party has dominated the political order during this time of increased social control over youths and has proven itself to be blind to sub-cultural differences and ethnic minority, class and gender inequalities.

The public should hold those in power accountable for their policies, programs and laws aimed at the social control of youth (see Kassebaum 1974). The question of whether government initiated reform measures actually reform youth is an empirical matter that deserves a fair, non-political assessment. As such, recent nation-wide changes in the education system should be carefully assessed by their ability to both reduce deviant youth behavior, including youth crimes, and to redress the inequality in the school system. These reforms were passed on the basis that such changes would reduce youth-adult conflict. A few years later, research should be conducted in order to discover if the reforms have positively impacted on student issues, such as violence and crime in the schools, absentee rates, etc., and juvenile delinquency rates preferably self-reported rates. Continuing research is especially needed regarding the inequality between schools. In the future, we should pay more attention to the anti-school subculture, the class and ethnic composition of students in those subcultures, and assess the impact that the reform measures have on it.

A final word

The biggest challenge is to raise public awareness about the problems faced by the youth of today; to create a picture of their lives that is not tainted by the dictates of politics and power. The public remains ignorant about the proliferation of adult controls over youths and the damage this has caused. Class, ethnic group and gender inequality remain taboo subjects and disadvantaged youths continue to have no where to turn for help. Regrettable, too, is that government and private funding supports the research and careers of academics who reinforce the 'status quo' perspective. This results in there being a lack of criticism against the power and ethnocentrism that emanates from the myth of Japan as an egalitarian *tan itsu minzoku* (homogeneous nation). The real tragedy though is the loss of potential among youths that, just because of their disadvantaged backgrounds, are unable to provide Japan with the innovation and greater acceptance of differences it needs to promote social diversity and progress.

Appendix 1: Notes on Methodology

Fieldwork

My research into youth crime began in 1983 and was for my Ph.D. dissertation (Yoder 1986). Time was initially spent with Japanese researchers at the National Police Science Research Center in Tokyo. Invaluable information was obtained on delinquency prevention, ecological features of misbehavior rates, and what the literature and researchers there purported as leading causes of pre-delinquency in Japan. Observations then took place on the streets. Through this research center, I was able to go along on and observe delinquency prevention patrols.

I accompanied plainclothes police and adult volunteers on a patrol in Shinjuku's entertainment district, a well-known youth hangout in Tokyo. On this patrol, it became quite clear that youngsters were being stopped and questioned even though, in most cases, they had done nothing wrong. Observing the youths' reactions during questioning and talking with a few of them alone after their police contact, I was left with the impression that they resented having been hassled by the police. Some of them were obviously quite upset. It appeared that these delinquency prevention tactics were all about surveillance and catching young people doing something wrong, rather than preventing them from getting into trouble.

Later, information was collected on delinquency prevention activities in and around Minami and Hoku through the *chōnaikai* (community association) and from the *bōhankai* (crime prevention unit) in Minami. (There is no crime prevention unit in Hoku.) The local city offices provided information on delinquency prevention activities and talks were held with adults directly involved with pre-delinquent youth, such as counselors at the city's juvenile counseling center. I also attended a few patrols in both areas.

Minami had one of the most active delinquency prevention programs in Shonan. Community action against youth crime came from adult volunteer work associated with the Minami crime prevention unit (*bōhankai*), part of the Minami Community Association (*chōnaikai*) and the Youth League (*seishōnenkai*).

Within the neighborhood, a good number of homes served as police checkpoints (*bōhan renrakusho*), all such places displayed a sign advertising this fact in front of their home. All community delinquency prevention activity was coordinated with the police and city juvenile delinquency prevention organization.

Not only did I go on patrols in Minami, but also in Kaigan. Unlike Minami, there are no delinquency prevention patrols in Hoku. There are, however, delinquency prevention patrols in other areas of Kaigan and one afternoon was spent going on a patrol with a plainclothes policeman and adult volunteers in Kaigan. These guidance patrols go to places where it is suspected that youths misbehave such as hidden areas near or in temples, shrines and at game centers.

The police and volunteers are looking to catch youths mis-behaving, while the youths are watching out for these patrol members. As we walked into one game center the youths hurriedly displayed their best behavior, all trying to look attentive while playing the machines. One volunteer spotted a boy smoking, with a packet of cigarettes in the shirt pocket of his school uniform. The policeman gave the boy a lecture and 'wrote him up' for smoking.

Even though casually dressed, young people still suspected that these adults had come into the game center to catch them smoking or doing something wrong. They took evasive action and the only reason one boy was caught smoking was because he was too slow in putting out his cigarette and removing the packet from his front pocket. Guidance patrol members played the role of law enforcers as they looked for young people committing crimes. Young people in the game center played the role of 'look outs' for guidance workers. There is, however, one obvious major difference: the police had the power to enforce the law while the young people had the law against them. Thus, when the young boy was caught smoking, there was little he could do but to at least give the appearance of agreeing with the lecture the policeman gave him.

Once familiar with delinquency prevention in both areas, I began observing youth behavior in an entertainment district located near

Minami in Shonan. Anyone hanging around entertainment districts can see what is happening there and I played the role of a detached observer. This meant going to places popular among youths, watching what they do and then recording what I observed.

Nearby Minami, I went to game centers, *pachinko* (gambling) parlors, drinking places, fast food joints, coffee shops and hung around street corners popular among youths. Becoming familiar with the context, interactions and actions of misbehavior and the things young people did for fun was very useful in my later interviews with Minami and Hoku youth.

As detailed in Chapter 2, I also visited the local middle schools. The reluctance of school officials at the Minami middle school to allow me to visit and the way they whisked me out when I did finally go there strongly suggested that they did not want anyone to know what goes on in their school. In contrast, the immediate invitation and co-operative discussions I had with school officials at the Hoku local middle school reflected their openness and pride in the school.

Interviews, talks and survey research

Letters were sent out to the mothers of each Minami youth asking permission to interview their child. The initial response was dismal. However, subsequent door-to-door contacts, telephone follow-ups and word of mouth created a snowball effect and resulted in most youths being interviewed (see Yoder 1986).

In Hoku, as in Minami, an attempt was made to interview all youth. The procedure for scheduling interviews, however, proceeded somewhat differently. A letter was first sent to all the youth mothers, asking permission to interview their child. However, instead of sending another letter and then going around door-to-door, my Japanese wife telephoned the homes of non-respondents. Being a mother (we had two small children at that time) in the community helped her to convince other mothers to agree to allow their children to be interviewed. Door-to-door follow-ups and questionnaires sent to non-respondents followed in the same way as in Minami.

The eighty-three percent response rate (132 of 159) obtained in both communities was very high for social research in Japan. The main reason for this high response rate was persistence. Through a very time consuming, step-by-step procedure, I gradually gained the trust of most parents and their children. As the interviews proceeded people became less suspicious of my motives. The fact that I was an American and was therefore perceived as an outsider, as someone who posed no threat, also encouraged them to participate and to speak their minds.

Conducting follow-up studies

The two follow-up studies were independent research conducted by myself. The first follow-up study in 1987 involved only one set of questionnaires being sent to the homes of all the youths that I had interviewed in the original study (two Minami youths interviewed in the original study were excluded because of their mothers' presence during the interview.) Potential respondents were instructed to fill out the questionnaire (and a pen was put in the envelope) and post it back to my home address in the stamped envelope provided. At that time, my family was relocating to California and further follow-up of non-respondents was not possible.

The second follow-up study from 1998 to 1999 was far more thorough and endeavored to discover what had become of each youth that I had interviewed fourteen or fifteen years earlier. The former Minami youths, now young adults, were sent a very detailed questionnaire (63 questions) to their original home address; a pen and stamped envelope with my address was enclosed with all questionnaires. Even though I suspected that most of the youths/ young adults would have moved, I hoped most of their parents still resided in the neighborhood and would make sure their child got the mailed questionnaire. When the family had moved (indicated on the mailed envelope sent back), a change of address was checked-on through a most reliable source. Then, among those that did not return the questionnaire or moved to a known change of address, two more questionnaires at different times and shorter in length were sent out. Finally, in the summer of 1998, the original homes and in some cases the homes that either the family or former youth had moved to of all non-respondents were visited. A few informants also helped to get information on the non-respondents.

Questionnaires were sent to the home addresses of the original Hoku youths (by then, young adults) on July 31st, 1998. The long-version questionnaire had been shortened to twenty-four questions so as to increase the response rate. Similar to Minami, records were made available to find current addresses for those who moved. In the middle of September, a second shortened questionnaire was sent out to all non-respondents. Then, from February 1999 to late March, all the homes of the Hoku non-respondents were visited.

Reliability and validity

The follow-up studies served as a reliability check on the original study as later information could be compared with the earlier interviews. For example, in the original study youths recorded their misbehavior on a misbehavior checklist (acts of youth crime or status offenses). Then in the first and second-follow-up study they were asked to recall their adolescent misbehaviors. If they reported smoking at fourteen in the original study, then they should also have reported smoking again at about the same age on the misbehavior checklist in the first follow-up study. Most were consistent in self-reporting of misbehavior acts and age of first engaging in such acts. Other responses (background information, school particulars, etc.) in the follow-up studies closely matched the information provided in the original interviews. While there were many checks on the reliability of information during the original research (matching questions, comparison of sibling responses, post-interview checklists, participant observation, etc.) matching responses over time enhanced the credibility and reliability of information obtained in the original interviews. This also lent confidence to the reliability or 'truth' of information received in both of the follow-up studies.

Following changes over time added meaning (validity) to the research. A response at one point in time depends on the individual's feelings, mood and most recent experiences. This then creates the uncertainty as to whether or not, if interviewed on another day the respondent might feel quite differently about the same issue. However, by asking the same question at two points in time I was able to correct for this problem and thereby add greater substance to the responses.

To sum up the fieldwork, primary attention was given to observing ecological conditions and situations of youth crime, then tracking over time the consequences of youth deviance on a young person's transition into early adulthood. These situations and conditions were controlled for in a longitudinal field experiment panel design: one area (Minami) was considered delinquency-prone while the other area (Hoku) was not. Youth behavior (including crime) was observed as it took place and information was obtained and observations made on ecological features (mainly play areas, schools, community life and delinquency prevention activities) and interpersonal relations (e.g., youth-parental attachment) relevant to the social life and behavior of Minami and Hoku youths. Changes over time were followed-up through further observations of these former youths to see what had become of them and how their past behavior and the ecological features of youth crime (area and class background) related to their social economic status as young adults.

Fieldwork and data gathering techniques

My fieldwork utilized a number of data gathering techniques to describe the contexts and meanings of youth behavior. A short discussion of the characteristics of each research technique follows.

1) Naturalistic observation of youth behavior in Shonan entertainment district

Naturalistic observation means that the fieldworker observes behavior as it occurs in a natural setting but does not interfere with what's going on nor get involved with the persons observed. At the beginning of this naturalistic observation component of my fieldwork I needed to find out where young people hung-out in the entertainment district and what they did at these places. So, unobtrusively, I tracked their movements and re-visited these places time and time again.

A good fieldworker observes and notes everything, no matter how trivial it may seem. Hence, I noted what youths were wearing, how many of them there were, whether they were alone or with friends, what they were doing and the general atmosphere (including physical layout) of the places they frequented. Street observations commonly took place on one particular street corner where motorcycles and cars were the center of attraction for young people. Notes were made into a small notepad as soon as I turned the corner. From the moment of getting off the train station in Shonan (entertainment district adjacent to the station) to leaving the area, I gave my full attention to anything and everything relating to youth.

From 1 September 1983 to 31 August 1984 I spent one hundred and five days observing youth behavior in the Shonan entertainment district. These observations were made in the evening, often quite late. After awhile, I began to participate in the same activities as the youths, playing video games and *pachinko* hanging out here and there and so on along with everybody else. Knowing about these places and happenings helped me gain rapport with the youths during the interviews and reduced suspicion among the employees and proprietors of these shops as to why a foreigner kept frequenting such establishments; I have never seen a foreigner hangout at such places. Still, caution was taken not to get too involved. Notes were made about this involvement and other changes that I was going through while the study progressed. It must be remembered that fieldworkers too are changed by the setting their involvement with people and situations and that this influences what they observe and how they interpret it.

2) Talks with people involved in delinquency prevention and going on patrols

At the beginning of the research, contacts were made with various people associated with delinquency prevention in Shonan and Kaigan. I wanted to have some idea what these people did to make an assessment of how such actions could prevent youth crime and what these activities meant to the youths. While such persons were very helpful in providing information and allowed me to go on patrols with them, it had to be made clear that the research was about youth not adult delinquency controls. A few adults associated with delinquency prevention in Minami suggested that I focus on what teachers and parents thought were the problems of youth crime. When I mentioned my intention to interview youths, a few members of the local Minami crime prevention association objected and did not like what I was doing. Also, so that the youths would not assume that I supported or was associated with delinquency prevention, once I began interviewing them I ended all contact with members of delinquency prevention organizations.

3) Interviews with youths during the original study and talks with them and others (usually parents) during the second follow-up study

Details on interviews in the original study are covered in my dissertation (Yoder, 1986). Questions were open-ended and constructed on the basis of my review of youth crime literature and from participant observations in the field. All interviews were conducted alone with the youth and were tape-recorded. Interviews lasted from forty-five minutes to over two hours.

I found it very important to identify, to gain rapport, with whoever was being interviewed. This was crucial to encouraging youths in the original study and later when they were young adults in the second follow-up study or the parent(s) of non-respondents when going door to door in the second follow-up study, to open up.

4) Measurement of family social class

In the original study, a father's occupation and mother's working status were the main indicators of family social class. Parents' education was added to the picture in the first and second follow-up studies. In both Minami and Hoku there were some cases where parental education remained unknown. In Minami, when a parent's education was not known, the father's occupation, mother's working status and living condition (condition of their home or apartment) was used to indicate a middle or lower working class family background.

In Hoku, to be included in the upper class, both parents' had to be college graduates or father a college graduate and mother a special school graduate. There was only one exception to this, a boy whose father was a wealthy landowner with an aristocratic family background.

Most Hoku fathers were businessmen in middle to large prestigious Japanese companies. This created a problem in distinguishing middle from upper class occupations, since youths either did not know or did not want to say exactly what position their father held in a company. Thus, I assumed that fathers' with a college education held managerial positions. This assumption was somewhat validated by the mother's working status. Mothers not working suggested financial well being and thus that their husbands held a reasonably high position within a company. When the father was a businessman, upper class families were distinguished from middle class families by mother's working status and her educational and professional working background. In upper class families, all mothers were housewives or worked as professionals and all but one (the one exception being a wife of a wealthy landowner) of these mothers had either a college degree or graduated from a special school.

In the cases where parents' education was not known in Hoku, the father's occupation and the family's standard of living, as indicated by the amount of land they owned and the quality of their home, was used to distinguish middle and upper class families. If the father was a professional then they were considered to be upper class families. However, when the father was a businessman and the mother didn't work, upper or middle class status was determined by the size of land and quality of the home they lived in; if the mother worked they were considered middle class. Being conservative here, their home had to be of a higher quality than most homes of Hoku youths, which were all quite nice. Inclusion into the upper class required that the family had one or more homes on their land and the main home was a high quality, two-story house located on a large property.

5) Case studies

During the original study I selected a handful of youths with which I met a number of times either for interviews or less formal talks and one-on-one get-togethers. In all cases, the youth and I became quite close. These case studies did not just involve an exchange in a lot of information, but also the sharing of feelings, moods and the revelation of quite personal details. Although I sided with and became attached to these young people, I maintained a certain distance and on a few occasions declined to take part in certain activities that would have crossed the line in our relationship. Also, as best as I could, I tried to be a positive influence on their lives by showing that someone cared about them. These experiences were quite touching and opened my eyes to the adolescent world, with all its complexities and varieties. I feel very indebted to these young people.

6) Making, sending out and monitoring returns of questionnaires in all three studies

The whole process of making, sending out and monitoring the return of questionnaires was extremely tedious and time consuming, yet was a major part of the research, particularly for the follow-up studies. In the original study, questionnaires were sent to youths that did not want to or could not be interviewed. In the first follow-up study, only one set of questionnaires was sent to the youths that had been interviewed three to four years earlier. For the second follow-up study, three sets of questionnaires were sent to former Minami youths, now young adults, and two sets of questionnaires to their Hoku counterparts. Also, door-to-door inquiries were made at the homes of all non-respondents in the second follow-up study.

The original study was a total survey of all Minami and Hoku youth. The questionnaires covered the same topics as the interviews, though in less depth, and were sent to the interview non-respondents. Fifty-eight percent (18 of 31) of Minami and sixty percent (21 of 35) of Hoku youths who did not respond to the request for an interview completed and returned the questionnaire. Data in questionnaires and interviews were compared, with no significant differences detected. In Minami, eighty-two percent of all youths were either interviewed or completed a questionnaire and in Hoku the figure was eighty-four percent. This high response rate in a total survey lends credence to a claim that responses to my inquiries (interviews and questionnaires) were representative of all youth residing in both Minami and Hoku.

The two follow-up study questionnaires were similar in content to the original interview with additional questions asking about the respondent's present-day life. Nearly half of the youths residing in Minami and Hoku responded to the first follow-up questionnaire. Forty-one percent (16 of 39) of Minami young adults responded to the first, second or third questionnaire during the second follow-up study. Information on another thirty-six percent (14 people) of Minami youths was obtained by talks with them or their parent(s); in one case information came from an informant. This made for a total response rate of seventy-seven percent. Forty-five percent (23 of 51) of Hoku youth responded to the first or second questionnaire during the second follow-up study. (One youth had died in an automobile accident.) Information was obtained on another thirty-nine percent (20 people) from talks with them or their parent(s). This resulted in an eighty-four percent response rate. A few individuals in Minami and Hoku were both interviewed and completed questionnaires during the second follow-up study.

Information was not obtainable on less than twenty percent of all the youths originally interviewed. The reason for this was that either they could not be found (i.e., they had moved without providing a forwarding address) or did not respond to questionnaires sent to their new address (that, in all cases, was outside of either Minami or Hoku).

The status of nine Minami young adults interviewed in the original study is not known and missing data occurred in one case. These young people could not be located or did not respond to both the first and second follow-up studies. The pattern of transition from adolescence to early adulthood for Minami youths (described in Chapters 4 and 5) in all likelihood would not have been much different had follow-up information been obtained from these missing young adults. The original interviews with them indicated that they had a similar experience of adolescence as those that were contacted in the follow-up studies. For example, among these nine non-respondents, those at low ranked high schools had the same troubles and reported high rates of misbehavior as respondents to the follow-up studies.

The absence of follow-up information on these nine non-respondents does, however, mean that I have underestimated the amount and varieties of youth-adult conflict among Minami youth; information from them would have, in all likelihood, painted an even more tumultuous picture of the transition from adolescence to early adulthood. Four lower working class non-respondents were very active in misbehavior and three were associated with a youth gang. It is reasonable to speculate that troubles with the law or deviant lifestyles contributed to my inability to contact them later in life.

In Hoku, during the second follow-up study, I was unable to locate eight of the original youths. With the exception of two females who were fairly active in misbehavior, the adolescent lives of these eight non-respondents were very similar to those of the other forty-three respondents.

Of the five female non-respondents, three attended higher ranked private all-girls high schools, something characteristic of Hoku female adolescents. None of the eight non-respondents attended a low ranked high school. Of the three males, at the time of the original study, one was attending an upper ranked high school, another went to an upper-ranked private all-boys middle school and the third boy was a student at the local middle school. All but one non-respondent (her father died when she was in high school) came from a two-parent family and all came from middle or upper class families. Of the three (all females) that had graduated from high school, two were attending a special school and one was a junior college student.

In summation, there were no significant differences between these eight non-respondents and the forty-three youngsters accounted for in the second follow-up study. Thus, the deviant youth behavior and the transition from adolescence to early adulthood for Hoku youth described in this book is representative of all Hoku youth.

7) Talks with community members in Minami and Hoku

Throughout this field study, numerous conversations have taken place with Minami and Hoku adults. As one would expect, I got along better with some of these adults than with others. For example, one small shop owner in Minami during the original study and then fourteen years later in the second follow-up study has been very helpful in letting me know about happenings in Minami. Conversely, a few adults active in delinquency prevention in Minami did not like what I was doing (e.g., interviewing youths) and our relationship was decidedly cold. During all three studies, I gave my phone number and home address to all parent(s) and youths mentioning that they could contact me at any time. Making myself available and showing appreciation for their help was important to gaining trust with all these people.

8) Keeping up with changes in Minami and Hoku

Since 1991, except for one year living in Tohoku (northern Japan) and a year residing in a city near Shonan, I have lived in Kaigan. I quite frequently return to Shonan and Minami and keep up with the changes there. Shonan and Kaigan, and particularly Minami and Hoku, are places where I feel quite comfortable and, remarkably, little has changed in these two communities and cities since this study began twenty years ago.

Appendix 2: Youth Perspective on Youth-Adult Conflict

Youth perspective on conflict with adults

Young people are more aware of causes and solutions to youth problems than adults give them credit for. It is obvious, yet overlooked, that if we want to know why youths get into trouble that we should ask them. During the original interviews, young people were asked if they thought parents, teachers, neighbors or the police could understand the problems of youth. They also were asked if there was a generation gap in Japan.

All five questions about youth-adult problems were open-ended and encouraged the respondents to freely speak their mind. Each question used the same word order and grammatical style. For example, the first question was, 'Do you think parents can understand the problems of youth'? Then, the next question was, 'Do you think teachers can understand the problems of youth'? Whatever the reply (with typical responses being 'I think so,' 'to some extent' or 'I don't think so'), they were asked to explain their response. Responses were then arranged in an ordinal ranking from yes, somewhat to no.

There were differences of opinion as youths in the most negative and stringent social control situations (i.e., Minami youth attending low ranked high schools) were far more vehement in their objections to the social control establishment. Still, a majority of all youth did not think adult social control agents (parents, teachers, neighbors and police) could understand youth problems (see Yoder 1986: 248).

The only question that significantly divided the youths' responses related to the ability of teachers to understand youth problems. Twice as many youths that attended low ranked high schools compared to those that attended higher ranked schools replied 'no' to the question, 'Do you think teachers can understand youth problems'?

The greatest consensus was with regard to the generation gap, with eighty-eight percent of all youths replying 'yes,' eight percent 'somewhat' and only four percent 'no' to the question of the existence of a generation gap (Yoder 1986:254).

Quantitative results are less important than the substance of youths' responses to these questions. Few youngsters blamed youth for youth-adult misunderstanding or generation conflict. The majority opinion was that adult controls over youths aren't working because adult social control agents fail to understand what youth are all about. In accordance with what is presented in this book, young people identified 'labeling' and negative adult controls as the primary sources of youth-adult conflict. What follows are examples of the comments made in response to these questions.

Many youths thought adults couldn't understand them simply because they were no longer young. Age difference contributes to parents' misleading notions of juvenile delinquency. One young person said, 'They aren't youth themselves, so their way of thinking is different. For example, the causes they give for juvenile delinquency are those that I think aren't related to the issue at all' (Yoder 1986:249).

The mass media has long waged a negative campaign against youth crime. They blow-up a few sensational youth crimes and then insinuate that something is wrong with all youth. The mass media has been supportive of adult delinquency control measures, broadcasting official (police and politicians') opinions on youth deviance while ignoring a youth perspective. One young person that I interviewed blamed the mass media for making matters worse.

Of course youngsters must do something to solve their problems but parents are bad, too. Well not only the parents the people in mass communication are the worse. I don't like them. I think they always enlarge the problem (Yoder 1986:256).

Young people thought adults contributed to the problem of juvenile delinquency. Adults expect trouble from young people, so that is exactly what they selectively choose to look for and find. Adults do not try to understand youth, but rather label them as 'bad,' not paying attention to what that particular youth is all about. As the comments below show, many young people felt that adults' labeling of youth was a cause of youth deviance (Yoder 1986: 251–253, 256–258).

About teachers labeling students, various youths had this to say:

> If teachers find students doing something bad, they just punish them. They don't try to understand the student's mind. They say to the student['s] it's not a good thing to do but don't ask them why they did it. They just say "you have done a bad thing," and don't show students any example about how to live.

> A girl in the [school] marathon was tired and running behind everybody. The teacher said well, she must have sniffed glue. That is a really bad [thing to say] and looking at teachers this way I can't trust them.

> They [teachers] show favoritism, treating good students nicely and rejecting those who even show a slight bit of deviancy.

About police labeling youth, the following comments were made (Yoder 1986 252,253):

> Police are too restrictive. I think they are more restrictive now than before. Parents and the police are like judges. They judge a person by his appearance, don't they. They don't try to see the inside.

> I somehow don't like the police. Even if you don't do anything bad they suspect you of doing something without giving you a chance to explain.

> The police do not understand [youth problems]. When you do something 'bad' they insist you are wrong.

A Minami boy felt that neighbors give youths negative labels.

> The neighbors are prejudiced. If they decide that a youth is 'bad' then he is thought of only as a person who does bad things. They do not recognize anything else about that youth except that he is a "bad person." (Yoder 1986:253)

Some youths felt that adults needed to relax their zealous ways of controlling youths in order to reduce youth-adult conflict and even questioned the adult definition of youth crime (Yoder 1986: 256–258).

The society as a whole is fussy about delinquency. For example, many parents worry easily if their children should become a delinquent if their children smoke a little. They should believe their children, and leave them alone. I think they tend to be excessively protective. As the society is fussy about delinquency parents tend to point out their children's trivial conduct. They should watch at a distance without saying anything and if their children fail at something they should give them advice instead of telling them: "I told you so."

Few parents trust their children and it is those children feeling so deserted that become delinquents. If parents trust their children, delinquency will decrease.

Instead of telling us to do this and that encourage the children to think and act on their own.

I don't want them to judge what is wrong before having a discussion with us.

I don't want them [adults] to judge us by their standards and I want them to respect our way of thinking.

I want them to talk to us. Yes, we are responsible people too. I wish they would listen to us before they speak. We are the same human beings so I would like them [adults] to remember that they were once the same age, and I want them to talk to us on an equal basis.

I don't want them to see things from a single perspective. I want them to see things from many different angles.

One should appreciate the children individually and not view them collectively as children. The adults today think of middle school students as a collective group but they [the students] are all unique. For example, girls, A, B, and C all have their own personalities, so one has to view them separately like girl A is this way, B is another way, and C has her own way as well. I want them to recognize and appreciate each person's individuality.

It's not necessary that they keep saying things are bad. We know. Youth are as stupid as adults think.

At least from the early 1970s, adult social control measures against youth have increased. This partially accounts for the dramatic rise of arrests and guidance rates of juvenile delinquency from the 1970s to 1980s (and increasing again from the early 1990s). Greater official attention and surveillance of youth has resulted in the obvious: more kids have been caught and punished for 'doing something wrong'.

This 'war on youth' has been initiated by political leaders and has resulted in the implementation of increased coercive measures (including laws). These leaders are invariably old and most, in their own youths, received militarist indoctrination that glorified the uniqueness and superiority of Japanese ways. They have the greatest access to and control over the mass media and have a profound influence on public perceptions and opinions regarding youth problems. The older generation is prone to believe in these political leaders and cling-on to the past ways of handling youth dissent. Many youths blamed today's generation gap on the pre-war thinking of the older generation. The following are poignant comments made by two young people about this very different way of thinking between adults and youths (Yoder 1986: 255).

The adults may or may have not lived through war but all of them more or less have that period in common, so their thinking lacks freedom and is bound by rules. For example, they say one should obey one's parents, the father is the most important figure in the family, you have to obey your teachers and they [teachers] are always right. Our parents have been brought up in such a way of thinking which is very different from the children [youth in Japan today] in the present free society.

The parents these days belong to the post-war generation, when things were scarce. Now we have affluence. Japan at that time was a defeated nation and they still have that image of the country, and they all had war-time military education to a certain extent. They didn't quite join the army but they had military education in the elementary schools. They still have that image of Japan. But we [youth] view Japan in a more calm way. Japan is a big nation today, although it's only her economy and the natural resources are limited. I think parents are more fanatical about Japan than we are.

Appendix 3: Concept and Rates of Pre-delinquency

Pre-delinquency

Pre-delinquency covers status offenses or 'crimes' that only apply to youth. Pre-delinquency is set in juvenile law and youth are liable for punishment should they be caught in violation of any one of numerous status offenses. In Japan, there are two categories of pre-delinquent juveniles: crime-prone juveniles and misconduct juveniles. Cases of police guidance, given to youth under the 'label' of crime-prone juveniles are very small in number (less than one percent of pre-delinquent offenders), representing what the authorities believe are the more serious cases of pre-delinquents and repeat offenders.

The number of youths cited for pre-delinquent or misbehavior offenses are far greater than those cited for committing any other category of crime. The most recent figures, for 2001 (Hanzai Hakusho 2002; Seishōnen Hakusho 2002), reveal that police

Table A3.1   Guidance rates and misconduct violations

Reason for Police Guidance	Number	Population Percent per 1,000 Youth
Penal Code Offenses	198,939	14.5
Misconduct	971,881	70.6
Misconduct Violations	**Number**	**Percent**
Smoking	473,988	45.1
Roaming around late at night	370,523	38.1
Bad companionship	35,177	3.6
Gang activity	32,220	3.3
Drinking	30,577	3.1
Other	65,396	6.7
Total	**971,881**	**99.9**

guidance for misbehavior was nearly five times greater than the second largest crime category or juvenile arrests for Penal Code Offenses. These figures and misbehavior offenses cited are provided in Table A3.1.

References

Adams, Thomas (1980), *Introduction to the Administration of Criminal Justice*, Englewood Cliffs, New Jersey: Prentice-Hall Incompany.

Ames, Walter L. (1981), *Police and Community in Japan*, Berkeley, California: University of California Press.

Andressen, Curtis and Peter Gainey (2002), 'The Japanese Education System: Globalisation and International Education,' *Japanese Studies* ,Vol. 22 (2), pp. 153–167.

Bayley, David (1976), *Forces of Order: Police Behavior in Japan and the United States*, Berkeley: University of California Press.

Chambliss, William J. (1975), 'The Saints and the Roughnecks', in Friedman (ed.,) *Annual Editions: Readings in Sociology*, Guilford, Connecticut: Dushkin Publishing Group, Inc..

Christopher, Robert C. (1984), *The Japanese Mind*, London and Sydney: Pan Books.

Clifford, William (1976), *Crime Control in Japan*, Lewington, Massachusetts: Lexington Books.

Cohen, Albert K. (1988), 'Reference Group Identification and Deviant Behavior,' in Farrell and Swiggert ed., *Social Deviance*, Third Edition. Belmont, California: Wadsworth Publishing Company.

Coleman, James William and Donald R. Cressey (1990), *Social Problems,* 4th Edition. New York, New York: Harper & Row Publishers Incompany.

Colvin, Mark and John Pauly (1988), 'Toward An Integrated Structural-Marxist Theory of Delinquency Production,' in Farrell and Swiggert ed., *Social Deviance,* Third Edition. Belmont, California: Wadsworth Publishing Company.

Condon, John C. (1984), *With Respect to the Japanese A Guide for Americans*, Yarmouth, Maine: Intercultural Press Inc..

Coser, Lewis, Steven L. Nock, Patricia A. Steffan and Buford Rhea (1987), *Introduction to Sociology,* second edition. Orlando, Florida: Harcourt Brace Jovanovich In-company.

Criminal Justice in Japan (pamphlet, no date), Tokyo: Ministry of Justice.

Cummings, William K. (1980), *Education and Equality in Japan*, Princeton, New Jersey: Princeton University Press.

Deutsch, Morton and Robert M. Krauss (1965), *Theories in Social Psychology*, New York, London: Basic Books, Inc..

DeVos, George A. (1973), *Socialization for Achievement*, Berkeley, California: University of California Press.

DeVos, George A. and Hiroshi Wagatsuma (1984), *Heritage of Endurance: Family Patterns and Delinquency Formation in Japan*, Berkeley, California: University of California Press.

Erickson, Erik (1978), 'Eric Erickson's Eight Ages of Man,' in *Readings in Sociology 78/79*, Guilford Connecticut: Annual Editions, the Dushkin publishing group inc..

Farrell, Ronald A. and Victoria Lynn Swigert, ed., (1988), *Social Deviance*, Third Edition. Belmondt, California: Wadsworth Publishing Company.

Foljanty-Jost, Gesine (2000a), 'Young Workers in Japan,' *Social Science*, (Newsletter of the Institute of Social Science, University of Tokyo)18:22–26.

.... (2000b), 'Heartful Guidance:Fighting Juvenile Delinquency in a Japanese Community,' Unpublished Manuscript.

Fujita, Hidenori (1995), 'A Crisis of Legitimacy in Japanese Education: Meritocracy and Crisis' in James J. Shields Jr., ed., *Japanese Schooling*, Fourth Printing. Pennsylvania: Pennsylvania State University.

.... (2001) 'The reform of the Japanese education system as an answer to delinquency'. Unpublished Manuscript.

Greenfield, Karl Taro (1994), *Speed Tribes*, New York: Harper Perennial.

Hanzai Hakusho (1998), *Heisei 10 ban Hanzai Hakusho* (Heisei 10, White Papers on Crime). Tokyo: homusho insatsu hakko.

.... (2002), *Hesei 14 ban Hanzai Hakusho* (Heisei 14, White Papers on Crime). Tokyo: zaimusho insatsu hakko

Henslin, James M. (2002), *Essentials of Sociology*, Fourth Edition, Boston: Allyn and Bacon.

Hood, Christopher P. (2001), *Japanese Education Reform*, London and New York: Routledge.

Hoshino, Kanehiro (1983), 'Applicability of American Etiological Theories on Crime to the Explanation of Crime in Japan.' Unpublished Manuscript.

Japan Times (2000) June 2, Tokyo: Japan Times.

.... (2002) June 25, Tokyo: Japan Times.

Kanazawa, Satoshi and Alan S. Miller (2000), *Order by Accident: The Origins and Consequences of Conformity in Contemporary Japan*, Colorado: Westview Press.

Kassebaum, Gene (1974), *Delinquency and Social Policy*, Englewood Cliffs, New Jersey: Prentice-Hall, In-company.

Keisatsu Hakusho (2002), *Keisatsu Hakusho Heisei 14* (Heisei 14 White Papers on Police), Tokyo: zaimusho insatsu hakko

Kiyonaga, Kenji (1982), '*Furyou koi shounen ni okeru hikouka*' (A study of the Delinquent Career Among Misbehaved Juveniles), National Institute of Police Science on the Research and Prevention of Crime and Delinquency Vol. 23 (1), pp.1–8.

.... (1983), '*Hyou ryuu*' (Drifting Youth), National Institute of Police Science on the research and Prevention of Crime and Delinquency pp. 38–40.

Koko Juken Annai (1999), *Koko Juken Annai* (Guide to High School Entrance Examination), Yokohama: Kanto Publishing Company.

Kreitz-Sandberg, Susanne (2000), 'Modes of Change and Matters of Continuity-Reforms in Japanese High Schools,' Unpublished Manuscript presented at the 2000 International Symposium on Educational Reforms & Teachers Education Innovation for the 21st Century, Tokyo: Waseda University.

Lebra, Takei Sugiyama (1976), *Japanese Patterns of Behavior*, Honolulu, Hawaii: University of Hawaii Press.

Letendre, Gerald K. (2000), *Learning to be Adolescent*, New Haven & London: Yale University Press.

Linden, Eric and James C. Hackler (1988), 'Affective Ties and Delinquency,' in Farrell and Swiggert ed., *Social Deviance*, Third Edition. Belmont, California: Wadsworth Publishing Company.

Liska, Allen E. (1987), *Perspectives on Deviance,* Second Edition, Englewood Cliffs, New Jersey: Prentice-Hall Inc..

Lofland, John (1969), *Deviance and Identity*, Englewood Cliffs, New Jersey: Prentice-Hall, In-company.

.... (1986), *Analyzing Social Settings: A Guide to Qualitative Observation and Analysis,* Second Edition, Belmont, California: Wadsworth Publishing Company.

McVeigh, Brian J. (2000) 'Education Reform in Japan: Fixing Education or Fostering Economic Nation-Statism,? in Eades, J.S., Gill, Tom and Harumi Befu (ed.,), *Globalization and Social Change in Contemporary Japan*, Melbourne: Trans Pacific Press.

.... (2002), *Japanese Higher Education as Myth*, London and New York: M.E. Sharpe.

Mizushima, Keiichi (1973), 'Delinquency and Social Change in Modern Japan,' in DeVos (ed.,), *Socialization for Achievement*, Berkeley: University of California Press.

Montgomery, Cindy (2002), *'Discipline and Deviance: How Parent and Teacher Expectations Influence School-based Youth Problems in Japan,'* Unpublished Manuscript.

Nakane, Chie (1970), *Japanese Society*, Los Angeles and Berkeley: University of California Press.

Okano, Kaori and Motonori Tsuchiya (1999), *Education in Contemporary Japan*, Cambridge, New York and Melbourne: Cambridge University Press.

Osamu, Mizutani (1998), 'Youth Under Siege In a World of Drugs,' *Japan Quarterly*, October-December, Volume 45(4), pp76–83.

Reischauer, Edwin O. (1977), *The Japanese*, The Belknap Press of Harvard University Press: Cambridge, Massachusetts.

Rohlen, Thomas P. (1983), *Japan's High Schools*, Los Angeles and London: University of California Press.

Saito, Takao (2001), 'Increasing Less Equal,' *Japan Quarterly*, July–September, Vol. 48(3), pp. 24–30.

Sato, Ikuya (1991), *Kamikaze Biker: Parody and Anomy in Affluent Japan*, Chicago: University of Chicago Press.

Sato, Toshiki (2001), 'Is Japan a 'Classless Society,' *Japan Quarterly*, April–June, Vol. 48(2), pp.25–31.

Schreiber, Mark (1997), 'Juvenile Crime in the 1990's,' *Japan Quarterly*, April–June, Vol. 44(2), pp.78–89.

Schur, Edwin M. (1971), *Labeling Deviant Behavior: Its sociological implications*, New York: Harper Row, Publishers, Inc..

Seishonen Hakusho (1999), *Heisei 11 nen ban Seishonen Hakusho* (Heisei 11, White Papers on Youth), Tokyo: zaimusho insatsu kyoku hakko
.... (2002) *Heisei 14 nen ban Seishonen Hakusho* (Heisei 14, White Papers on Youth), Tokyo: zaimusho insatsu kyoku hakko
Selltiz, Claire, Marie Jahoda, Morton Deutsch and Stuart W. Cook (1959), *Research Methods in Social Relations*, New York and Toronto: Holt, Rinehart and Winston, Inc..
Shikita, Minoru and Shinichi Tsuchiya (1992), *Crime and Criminal Policy in Japan*, New York: Springer-Verlag.
Steinhoff, Patrica G. (1984), 'Student Conflict,' in Krauss, Rohlen, and Steinhoff (ed.,) *Conflict in Japan*, Honolulu: University of Hawaii Press.
.... (1993), 'Pursuing the Japanese Police,' *Law & Society Review* 27(4),pp: 827–850.
Sugimoto, Yoshio (2003), *An Introduction to Japanese Society*, Second edition, United Kingdom: Cambridge University Press.
Sutherland, Edwin (1988), 'Differential Association' in Farrell and Swiggert (ed.), *Social Deviance*, Third edition, Belmont, California: Wadsworth Publishing Company.
Suttles, Gerald (1968), *The Social Order of the Slum: Ethnicity and Territory in the Inner City*, Chicago, Illinois: University of Chicago Press.
Taki, Mitsuru (2001), 'Changes in School Environment and Deviancy,' Unpublished Manuscript.
Takane, Masaaki (1979), *Sōzō Hōhō Gaku* (Creative Methodlogy), Tokyo: Kodansha modern new books.
Verba, Sidney et.al. (1987), *Elites and the Idea of Equality*, Cambridge, Massachusetts: Harvard University Press.
Vogel, Ezra F. (1980), *Japan as No. 1: Lessons for America*, Tokyo: Charles E. Tuttle Company.
Weiten, Wayne (2001), *Psychology: Themes and Variations*, Belmont, California: Wadsworth Publishing Company.
White Papers on Police (1984), Tokyo: Police Association.
Whiting, Robert (2000), *Tokyo Underworld: The Fast Times and Hard Life of an American Gangster in Japan*, New York: Vintage Books, Knopf Publishing Company.
Willis, Paul (1977), *Learning to Labor*, Columbia University Press: New York.
Woronoff, Jon (1981), *Japan the coming social crisis*, Tokyo: Lotus Press.
Yoder, Robert S. (1986), 'A Pattern of Predelinquency for Youth in Two Suburban Japanese Communities,' Ph.D. diss., University of Hawaii.
Yokoyama, Minoru (1989), 'Net-widening of the juvenile justice system in Japan,' *Criminal Justice Review*, 14(1) pp.:43–53.
.... (1997), 'Juvenile Justice: An Overview of Japan' in Winterdyk, John (ed.), *Juvenile Justice System*, Toronto: Canadian Scholars Press, Inc.
Yonekawa, Shigenobu (2001), 'Inequality in Family Background as a reason for juvenile delinquency,' Unpublished Manuscript.
Yoneyama, Shoko (1999), *The Japanese High School: silence and resistance*, London and New York: Routledge.

Index